Sending Out Roots

Helping Parents and Teachers to Share the Faith

Carole M. Eipers

VERITAS

Published 2010 by
Veritas Publications
7–8 Lower Abbey Street
Dublin 1, Ireland

publications@veritas.ie
www.veritas.ie

ISBN 978 1 84730 244 1

Scripture taken from the New Revised Standard Version Bible:
Catholic Edition © 1993 and 1998 by the Division of Christian
Education of the National Council of Churches of Christ in the
United States of America. Used with permission. All rights reserved.

10 9 8 7 6 5 4 3 2 1

A catalogue record for this book is available from the British Library.

Designed by Tanya M. Ross
Printed by Hudson Killeen, Dublin

Veritas books are printed on paper made from the wood pulp of
managed forests. For every tree felled, at least one tree is planted,
thereby renewing natural resources.

In Memory of Ray

Contents

Chapter I

'You give them something to eat' (Mark 6:37)

When I was a child, I shared a bedroom with my grandmother. In the afternoon, I would go to our room and see my grandmother sitting in her easy chair clutching her beads, her lips moving silently.

There was no need for me to ask, 'What are you doing, Grandma?' The Rosary was part of our family prayer and during October we would pray it together. No explanation was required: Grandma was praying and I did not disturb her.

As I grew older, I understood that while she was praying she was not only remembering the mysteries of Jesus' and Mary's lives, but connecting their stories with her own annunciations and crucifixions as well. She saw them as a piece.

When my father asked me if I would like to go for a drive on a Saturday, I did not need to ask, 'Where are we going?' Every Saturday he went to the neighbourhood parish to go to confession. It was no surprise that, when I was seven years old, I too would receive this sacrament.

My mother was elected publicity chair for the parish women's group. My father belonged to the parish men's Mission Club and helped run fundraisers for needy people. Both of my brothers were altar boys and eventually I became one of the sacristan's helpers. It was part of life that one used one's gifts for the parish community.

It was all very Catholic; my whole childhood revolved around the parish. My friends and almost all of our neighbours were Catholic and my school was Catholic too. Whatever my classmates and I learned about the faith in school we saw lived in our homes, among our friends and families and in our village. Life and faith were one; it was secure and clear, if a little insulated.

In our village there were many churches: Episcopalian, Methodist, Lutheran, Presbyterian and Catholic. Catholics did not enter any of the other churches and a great curiosity about them built up in me. I remember when the Lutheran church near our home was undergoing renovation. My friends and I snuck around and tried to peek between the boards to see inside. Maybe the Lutheran children did the same when the Catholic church was renovated!

After I graduated from college, I became a teacher. The Catholic Church's self-understanding had developed and we were called to be ecumenical – to work with other Christians towards unity, and short of that to work together in Jesus' name to do good in the world. I had learned about the Second Vatican Council and joined an Ecumenical Urban Task Force in the city where I taught. It was exciting and fulfilling work. Together Christians were making a difference in that city. We had projects to address poverty and its causes, we picketed against unjust labour practices and we confronted racism.

I was only a few hundred miles from my childhood home, but light years from the insulation that it provided – for better sometimes, for worse other times. Working together ecumenically was far easier than ecumenical discussions about our beliefs. So much had to be explained that never did before; so much needed to be articulated beyond the words that my childhood Catechism answers afforded me.

A few years later, my husband and I returned to the village where I grew up to raise our son – things had changed. Nicholas went to the Catholic school and I taught there, but some of his friends were not Catholic. Some of my and my husband's friends were not Catholic either. Some childhood Catholic companions had married people of other Christian Churches. We were expanding our understandings, but it was unsettling sometimes. No longer could we assume that everyone believed as we did and sometimes people even asked questions like, 'Why do Catholics do that?'

The 'Catholic' practices we took for granted could not be taken for granted anymore. Some children did not know the prayers that everyone once knew. Some had one parent who was Catholic and another who was Presbyterian and they wanted to know the difference between these Churches and their beliefs. Others were suspicious of anyone who wasn't Catholic.

In this milieu I was a teacher. How often I wished I could have magical powers – as a teacher and a parent – in order to effectively promote growth in faith for those I taught!

Do you ever wish you had such powers? Not to gain money or power, but to share the Catholic faith. It would be so simple. We could reach to the heavens and catch that spark of faith. Then carry it carefully to our home, our parish, our neighbourhood, our workplace, our classroom – and ZAP! Infusing the knowledge that is the foundation for a relationship with Jesus Christ, and the conversion of heart and behaviour that follows, would be instantaneous and lasting. We could effect instant belief and hope and love, instant desire to learn about God, instant impetus to serve our neighbour.

Our work as parents and teachers would be accomplished once and for all. No recurring struggles as our children reach another age or have new questions; no doubts arising that would disturb our own faith; no battles about going to Mass.

Parents and teachers have often asked me about the ways they might 'hand on the gift of faith'. The good news here is that we recognise that faith is a gift from God. It is given; we have only to respond. The difficult part is that we look to 'hand it on' as we might hand on a family recipe. I often have the image of faith as a gift – a package wrapped in paper and tied with a bow. Wouldn't that be wonderful? We just take that gift box and 'hand it on' to our children, and it contains all that they need to know, believe and practise to be good Catholics.

If, indeed, you could hold that 'gift of faith' in your hands, boxed and bowed, ready to hand on to your children, what would be in it?

When I have asked this question of parents and teachers, they give a variety of answers. They name prayer, love of neighbour, Jesus' teachings, the commandments, hope, compassion for others, a sense of justice, forgiveness, or other dimensions of faith that are important. Sometimes Scripture is named, but not always. Then I ask, 'What are the uniquely Catholic elements you would want to include in that gift of faith you are handing on?'

It is interesting that until the second question is raised, the sacraments or the Mass are only occasionally mentioned. The second question also brings answers that include the pope, the bishops and Church teaching. What would be – or what *is* – in the gift of faith you are handing on?

We know that forming others – and growing ourselves – in faith is not as simple as handing over a wrapped package, nor are there magical powers available to enable us to do this most important work. Except – and it's a *big* except – we have faith and we have God's grace. And our God is certainly magical; after all, God created the sun and the moon and the stars. Moses encountered God in the burning bush. God led the Israelites through the desert with a pillar of fire by night. If only God would perform tricks like that today! Then we would have the spark of faith; then we could point to the works of God and our children would believe.

God could perform miracles like that today, of course. God could have 'zapped' all of us to assure we would always respond to his love positively. But that's not what God chose to do. Instead, God sent his only Son to become a human person. John's Gospel tells us, 'And the word became flesh and made his dwelling among us' (John 1:14). The all-powerful God sent his only Son, not in majesty, but in infancy; not with magical abilities, but with the love that works miracles. God became one of us and his coming transformed humanity.

The *Pastoral Constitution on the Church in the Modern World*, (*Gaudium et Spes*) from the Second Vatican Council tells us that the Son of God 'worked with human hands, he thought with a human mind. He acted with a human will, and with a human heart he loved. Born of the Virgin Mary, he has truly been made one of us, like to us in all things except sin' (GS 22).

Therefore, you and I do not need to wish for magical powers; we have the power of being sons and daughters of God, made in his image. We have the human abilities that Jesus did, now shot through with divinity and grace. We have all that we need to live and grow in our own faith and to assist others to grow in faith.

In Baptism we received the 'light of Christ'. Those baptised as adults heard the words, 'You have been enlightened by Christ. Walk always as children of the Light and keep the flame of faith alive in your hearts.' How do we walk 'as children of the Light'?

Years ago, before airline security tightened and limited how much baggage one could bring, I was travelling by plane to give a talk in another state. I was in line to board the plane, carrying only my Bible, as I needed to review the Scripture I was using in my presentation. In front of me were two women who had forty-two pieces of luggage between them: back packs, duffle bags, suitcases and huge handbags. Seeing them struggle and knowing their efforts would delay my boarding the plane, I offered to assist them. They gave me twelve pieces of luggage, or at least it seemed that many! We boarded and their seats were in the row just in front of mine. I helped hoist their luggage into the overhead compartment and then continued to my seat, still clutching my Bible. As I passed the two women to enter my row, one of them said to the other, 'No wonder she acts the way she does!'

They must have noticed me and my Bible! I was smiling, pleased. Then the other woman said, 'Yes, no one at work likes her, she's awful'. Alas, they were not speaking of me; but for one brief, shining moment, I thought my life was evidence of living the gospel. And, isn't that what is supposed to happen?

The key to nourishing others' faith is our own faith. When I ask parents and teachers about who helped them to grow in faith, they name grandparents and parents, teachers, priests and neighbours. When I pose the question, 'How did they help you to grow in faith?' there is always a strong element of witness. 'My mother was always reaching out to neighbours who were ill.' 'The teacher I had really showed what forgiveness means.' 'There was a girl who lived near me and she volunteered at the local hospital. She taught me about compassion.'

Think of the people who have helped you to grow in faith. Was it only with their words, or did their example prove the greater influence? If we are to spark faith, to hand on the gift of faith, to nourish young faith, we must be effective witnesses and more.

My grandmother set a good example as she sat quietly and prayed; because of the whole Catholic culture that enveloped me, she did not need words to explain her prayer. Today, in the midst of diversity and the variety of beliefs, perhaps we need both example and words. There are many people who sit and pray, some Christian, some our Jewish brothers and sisters, some of other faiths. We have to both do and be able to give voice to what we do and why we do it. The African community has a saying, 'You must walk the talk', when calling to witness. Today we are called to also 'talk the walk' in order to articulate our faith.

Many fine humanitarians do good works; when we do such works, it is in the name of Jesus Christ. That fact may not be evident unless we say it somehow. A study of young adults found they have great dedication to causes for peace and justice; the same study showed that many of them do not see any connection between their service to these causes and their faith. Perhaps they followed good example, but the words that make the connection were never uttered.

When we make a meal for a grieving family, or visit an elderly homebound person, do we tell our children Jesus is the reason? Faith is not only the source of good works for disciples of Jesus Christ, it is the sustenance which enables us to continue good works when the results are not immediate or even when our efforts seem to fail.

Jesus can only be our sustenance if we have responded to his call to be disciples, if we have experienced that conversion of heart that is necessary to embrace his teachings and to live as he asks. I saw a T-shirt recently that said, 'Change is good. You go first'. Conversion is change and, therefore, is not easy, but the reward is exceptional.

Jean Vanier, who founded the L'Arche community of disabled persons, described this reward when he said, 'The whole mystery of Christ is to change us so that we become the face of Jesus, we become the hands of Jesus, that we become the heart of Jesus, that our body becomes the body of Christ, that our words become the words of Christ' ('Seeing God in Others', aired on '30 Good Minutes', programme #3901, 7 October 1995). God's only Son became like us; we change to be like him and to proclaim his good news in word and deed to one another and to our children.

So, we have to change to become like Christ, to witness to our Catholic faith by our good deeds. We need to be able to share our faith in words as well so that others might grow in faith. We may feel like the disciples felt when Jesus preached to the huge crowd. Remember the story – the people had been there in the deserted place listening to Jesus for a long time and it was getting late. The disciples wanted Jesus to dismiss the crowd 'so that they can go to the surrounding farms and villages and buy themselves something to eat'. But Jesus says, 'You give them something to eat.'

In the midst of today's world, the hungers for faith and meaning, people – including our children – sit in the 'deserted places' of life and wait for nourishment. We may be tempted to point them to other places, to someone else who can satisfy their hungers, but Jesus says to you and to me, 'You give them something to eat'.

In John's Gospel, the story of the multiplication of the loaves includes a boy who had only five loaves and two fish to give to Jesus, and with these Jesus fed the multitude. We have talents, but they may seem meagre in the face of the overwhelming challenges of living and handing on the faith today. Yet, if we offer those abilities to Jesus, we become the instruments through which nourishment of faith can flow.

For Reflection

What talents and abilities do you have that help you to share your faith with others?

How will you 'feed' your own faith this year?

Tell the story of someone who helped you to grow in faith.

Chapter II

'What are you looking for?'
(John 1:38)

Technology's impact on relationships is stunning. Family members who are at a distance from one another can easily get in touch: there is e-mail, text messaging and other electronic services that allow us to speak to each other and even to see those who are physically far away. We can hold meetings online. We can access social networking sites and reconnect with friends and acquaintances we lost track of along the way. And, for those seeking love, there are dating sites that assure us we will find the perfect mate.

The commercials for dating sites explain the process one will engage in prior to meeting Mr or Ms 'Right'. One fills out a questionnaire giving pertinent information about oneself: age and education, profession and other interests. I understand some sites ask for a brief video so that potential partners can hear how an individual sounds and 'experience' what this person is like.

Presumably, after a choice of possible partners is made, there is a meeting, or perhaps several, to gain further knowledge of each other, to really experience each other in person. I would guess there is lots of conversation during these initial encounters. Then, if there is mutual interest, some other developments might take place: the couple might do an activity together that they discovered they both enjoy, for example, skiing or visiting an art museum. They learn to make choices based on common interests and values.

Eventually, the couple may celebrate the day they first met or a birthday or a holiday together. If the relationship has deepend, there will come the 'I'd like you to meet my family' time, the introductions of the partners to each other's community of relatives and friends. The couple may then join in with one of their families in a pet project that the family has always worked on: a parish fundraiser or a neighbourhood clothing drive. The new couple becomes part of the efforts of the families and their work in the world.

Of course, if you are not looking online for a partner, any new relationship may follow some of the same steps, but it can begin anywhere. For instance, I know people who found their future spouse among their sibling's friends; others met at school or in a workplace. Some met through a common interest in history or a sport. There are people who first met at a family gathering – a cousin brought a friend along and the relationship developed. A loving relationship can begin with casual conversation or at a celebration, in a shared leisure activity or in working side-by-side in an effort to promote peace. Think of one of your own loving relationships. How did it begin? How did it develop?

We might not think of growing in faith as a process of falling in love and deepening that love. Our own faith formation may have been focused on 'learning things' or our teachers may have taken for granted that we understood that the lessons and experiences were meant to help us to meet and love Jesus.

There is more to it, of course, than that beginning love. Just as in our loving human relationships the knowing, the conversing, the celebrating, the choosing, the shared community and common efforts to make things better for our families, our Church and the world continue to develop throughout our time together.

When two dear friends of mine first met, he was thirteen and she was twelve. She came along to a gathering with some girls he already knew. 'Who is *that* girl?' he asked. Now they are both in their eighties and they have been married for sixty-two years. She tends to his needs as he struggles with physical health issues and mental challenges. How much 'getting to know you' has happened since he first asked, 'Who is *that* girl?' How many conversations, how many celebrations, how many times did they base decisions for their growing family on shared values? Their community expanded beyond family and extended family to be too numerous to count. They have befriended people like themselves and others who are very different. They have worked to make life better for their families, their neighbourhood and the world through participation in countless hours spent in service.

When two of John the Baptist's disciples spotted Jesus walking nearby, they began to follow him. 'Jesus turned and saw them following him and said to them, "What are you looking for?" They said to him, "Rabbi" (which translated means Teacher), "where are you staying?" He said to them, "Come, and see"' (John 1:38-39). The disciples see Jesus, tag along, and Jesus notices them and asks, in effect, what they want. They want to know where he is staying. And then he gives them an invitation: 'Come, and see'. And they do. They go and spend the day with Jesus and then one of them, Andrew, goes and tells his brother, Simon Peter, about Jesus. Later Andrew brings his brother to Jesus.

I believe this story is one of immediate love, because John's disciples knew who they were looking for: the Messiah. They spent the day with Jesus and what a conversation it must have been! They learned from him and Andrew wanted to share Jesus with his family, so brought his brother to meet Jesus.

And so the gospel stories go: one encounter after another in which people meet and love Jesus and spend time with him. Their meetings with Jesus lead them to share the good news and to introduce others to the Messiah. When people encountered Jesus they lived differently.

The ways in which faith develops and love of God and neighbour grow remained consistent from the time of Jesus' life on earth through the era of the early Church. In the Acts of the Apostles, we read about the early Christians, who lived in the light of Jesus' resurrection and were strengthened by the presence of the Holy Spirit. 'They devoted themselves to the apostles' teaching and fellowship, to the breaking of the bread and the prayers' (Acts of the Apostles 2:42). The early Christians told the stories of Jesus and his teachings and those teachings dictated how they lived: they celebrated together, they prayed, they shared life in community and they witnessed to Jesus by the love they showed for God and neighbour.

As we help our children, youth and other adults to understand the gift of faith today, we do so in continuity with all those in the Scriptures, in the early Church and in the Church throughout the ages. We engage the same dimensions of formation in faith, the same development of love for God and neighbour that our own elders employed and that our ancestors in faith experienced, whether they encountered Jesus as he walked this earth or their encounter was mediated by the Christian community.

2/2173627

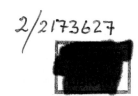

The *General Directory for Catechesis* assures us of the presence of those who have gone before us as we hand on the faith today: 'In truth, there is present in catechesis the faith of all those who believe and allow themselves to be guided by the Holy Spirit' (GDC 105). And the *Directory* tells us that when we teach the faith, we do so in the same ways that people have done it throughout the ages. 'Catechesis is nothing other than the process of transmitting the Gospel, as the Christian community has received it, understands it, celebrates it, lives it and communicates it in many ways' (GDC 105). In helping our children and each other to grow in faith, we are proclaiming the same Good News that Jesus himself proclaimed and that the saints proclaimed and lived, and they are with us as we teach today.

Who is with you when you hand on the faith? Not only these long ago ancestors, but surely those who introduced you to Jesus; those who first taught you to pray; those who celebrated with you at Mass and in the sacramental celebrations of your life; those who were part of the Christian community that formed you and those who work beside you in doing what Jesus asked us to do.

Whose faith influences your own, even as you share that faith with others? I was inspired by the faith of a young priest from the United States whom I met in the United Arab Emirates. He serves in Saudi Arabia, a country hostile to the Catholic Church, yet every day he risks his life to minister to Catholics in that country. My faith is also inspired by my friends, Ed and Kathy. Every day they witness to Jesus in small ways that make a difference. They bring a treat to someone who is homebound; they help an elderly neighbour shovel snow. I see their teenage daughters doing these same things now. Our faith can be influenced by those who do grand things and by those who offer tiny kindnesses in the name of Jesus.

We bring people to the love of Jesus Christ, and all that that love requires, in the same ways that we grow in love of any person. We engage in faith and share faith through the six dimensions of catechesis the Church reminds us of in the *General Directory for Catechesis*: knowledge, prayer, liturgical formation, moral formation, formation for community life and initiation into the mission of the Church.

We invite people to know Jesus Christ as we learn about him and teach about him. We pray and teach people to pray. We celebrate and enable others to participate in celebrating faith at Mass and in the sacraments. We follow Christ's teaching in the ways we live, speak, act and make decisions. We teach others by our words and witness how to make moral choices. We share life within a community of faith and introduce those we teach to the commitment that community life entails. We serve the mission of the Church in the world, sharing the Good News of Jesus Christ by our witness to gospel values and our care for those in need, and we make sure those we teach know that this mission is part and parcel of loving the Lord (see GDC 85–86).

When all of these aspects of faith formation are attended to, we know that there is a growth in our faith and we can see our children growing in their discipleship to Jesus Christ. My junior high students learned to pray long before they came to my class. They grew in prayer as we prayed together and with many different kinds of prayer. We participated in the liturgy together and they heard the call to go to love and serve the Lord. They knew about Jesus, because their parents had taught them and they deepened their knowledge of him as we reflected on Scripture. They learned to apply Jesus' teachings to their own lives and so to make loving choices.

As a community of faith, these young people made choices to serve. One of the ways they served was by going to Misericordia children's home to work with the mentally and physically disabled children who reside there. The students were amazing as they related to the children at Misericordia. They interacted with the children who were well enough to come to the gathering room and they did skits and crafts and fed the children who needed help eating. I watched the captain of our football team cradling a child and gently feeding him. Many of the children could not respond at all due to their conditions; they could not speak or smile. And yet, the students continued to go. They continued to be good news for children who were strangers to them.

One day we were planning our next visit to Misericordia and one of the students said to me, 'Some of us have been talking and we would like to be able to spend some time with the children who cannot leave their rooms'. I was in awe of their compassion and their willingness to reach beyond what they had known to visit children who were bedridden or attached to machines that made movement impossible. And so, on our next visit they went two-by-two to the children who were room-bound. Even the staff were amazed at these students and their interaction with the children.

My students had grasped and lived the mission of Jesus, but they had a further wisdom to share. When the students were preparing for graduation, they listed those people who should get an invitation to the ceremony: former teachers, priests who had served the parish but were no longer there, parents who had volunteered but had moved away. To that list the students added, 'Our friends at Misericordia'. Their outreach in service had also expanded their sense of community.

While the ways of forming in faith and living that faith find continuity with the past, our world is not the world of those who have gone before us. We do not wake up each day to life as Jesus knew it, nor to life as the early Christians knew it. Our hours are not filled with the same concerns that people who lived during the middle ages had. Our time is not even occupied in the same endeavours as those of our great-grandparents, or even those of our parents. And so the faith is handed on in continuity with the ways of the past, yet it must speak to the adults, youth and children of this time and place. For example, we still present Jesus' teaching to love our neighbour as we love ourselves. Today, that includes how we treat others in cyberspace.

After Jesus' resurrection, he met two of the disciples on the road to Emmaus. He asked them, 'What are you discussing with each other while you walk along?' (Luke 24:17). Amazed that this stranger (for they did not recognise Jesus) did not know of the events that took place in Jerusalem, they told him the story; they told him his own story. Then he told them the continuation of the story. First he listened, then he connected the new message to what they knew and had experienced. Ultimately, 'he was made known to them in the breaking of the bread'. Through the celebration, their vision was cleared and they knew Jesus.

Throughout Jesus' ministry on earth, he modelled how faith is taught. Using parables and examples or images that the people could understand, he taught them of God's love. He took their own experience and wove into it the message of faith, so that they could see, if not always accept, its implications for their daily lives.

What is life like for those with whom we share faith? What are their joys and sorrows? What makes them anxious or afraid? What are their dreams? It is only when we understand the answers to these questions that we can proclaim the Good News in ways that will make sense to them, ways that will answer the questions they have about life. Their life questions, and ours, are conditioned by many factors: age and development, education, experiences and cultural heritage. All of these factors play a role as we endeavour to share the faith with a particular person in a given moment.

Our vocation to share the faith, the vocation that comes from our Baptism and is expressed in our particular vocations as parents and teachers, is an awesome responsibility and sometimes a formidable challenge in today's world. But we have all that we need to fulfill that vocation. We have the gift of faith. We have God's grace and the inspiration that comes from the Holy Spirit. We have Jesus as our model of teaching. We have the example of all those who have gone before us in faith. We have the Church's wisdom to guide us in the ways that faith begins and grows: knowledge of the faith, prayer, liturgical formation, moral formation, education for community and initiation into mission (GDC 85, 86).

For Reflection

What are you looking for in your own faith this year?

In what situations have you 'recognised' Jesus' presence?

Interview an adult, youth or child to whom you teach the faith. Ask about their joys and anxieties. Listen.

Chapter III

'But who do you say that I am?'
(Mark 8:29)

Newspapers, magazines, television and the internet give us lots of information about famous people: politicians, actors, sports figures and ecclesial leaders. Most of us know something *about* the high-profile people in our world, but few of us really *know* them. In fact, I have heard people remark when a popular figure does something distasteful, 'I didn't know he was like that!' They might even say, 'I guess you just don't know some people'. We have limited knowledge of these famous people and since it is knowledge *about* them rather than knowledge *of* them, we cannot predict their behaviour.

Sometimes relationships begin with knowledge about someone. A friend or relative has someone in mind to whom they would like to introduce us. If the information they share piques our interest, we might express a desire to meet the person, to get to know them rather than just know about them.

In the document *On Catechesis in Our Time*, Pope John Paul II wrote, 'At the heart of catechesis we find, in essence, a Person, the Person of Jesus of Nazareth' (CT 5). He goes on, 'The definitive aim of catechesis is to put people not only in touch, but in communion, in intimacy with Jesus Christ' (CT 5). Clearly, as we attend to the task of giving people knowledge of the faith, it should be more than knowledge *about* Jesus. It should lead to an encounter with Christ and to continually developing in a loving relationship with him.

When you first meet a person and there is an initial attraction, what do you do? Many of us begin with conversation and asking questions: 'Where are you from?' 'Where did you study?' We might explore possible connections to other people: 'You know her too?' If we find mutual interest in pursuing the relationship, we will arrange to spend time together. In our time together we learn more, and the learning deepens our growing relationship.

When someone says, 'Tell me about yourself', what do you say? Introductions may scratch the surface of who we are right now. We might say something about where we live and what work we do. If we meet at some event we will perhaps identify who invited us or what our interest is in the event. If we progress in the conversation, we might hear, 'Tell me more about yourself'. What do you say then? Pushed to reveal more of ourselves we might talk about our families or some of our accomplishments in life. It is always interesting when someone says, 'Well, my uncle says you have a great sense of humour' or, 'My sister says you are a really good cook'. A new acquaintance may even tell us, 'I have been watching you at this gathering and I can tell that you are very good with elderly people'.

There are lots of ways we can gain knowledge about and knowledge of another person. We can listen to what others say about the person; we can watch the ways in which others react to the person; we can listen to what the person says; we can see how the person acts; we can engage the person and ask what he or she is thinking.

In literature, these are the ways in which an author reveals a character to us. They are known as the devices of characterisation. The Scriptures are God's self-revelation. We can know God because God has told us who he is. He has shown us who he is through his creation and through his words and actions. We also learn about God through reading in Scripture about the ways people reacted to him and what they said of this God.

God's greatest self-revelation is in his only Son. We can come to know Jesus by using the devices of characterisation to examine the gospels. We can also use the devices as a way to share the person of Jesus Christ with others.

Many people had a lot to say about Jesus before he was born. Throughout the Old Testament from God's promise to send a saviour, to the history of the chosen people's waiting, to the prophets who foretold his coming, we learn about the expected Messiah. Isaiah told of the Messiah who would be named, 'Wonderful Counsellor, Mighty God, Everlasting Father, Prince of Peace' (Isaiah 9:5). What do these titles mean to us as we come to know Jesus?

The expectation for the Messiah grew, it seems, with each generation. And, as the time of his coming approached, the angel Gabriel said to Mary, 'And now, you will conceive in your womb and bear a son, and you will name him Jesus' (Luke 1:31). A boy-child, who will be named Jesus, will be born of a woman, but this birth is different for 'the child to be born will be called holy; he will be called Son of God' (Luke 1:35).

The Word became flesh; the Incarnation of God's only Son is the fullest expression of God's love. And throughout the gospels Jesus reveals himself, and in revealing himself he reveals who God is.

Let us reflect on this Jesus in the gospels and what he reveals through his words and actions, through what others say about him and how they react to him, and, finally, through what he thinks and feels.

If we approach Scripture using the devices of characterisation, we can learn so much about Jesus. We can come to know who he was and is, what he taught, how people embraced or rejected him, and what he requires of those who would be his disciples.

We can look first to what Jesus says during his life on earth. Each gospel records different 'first' words of Jesus. In the Gospel of Matthew, the first words of Jesus are spoken as Jesus is seeking Baptism from John. Jesus says, 'Allow it now, for this it is fitting for us to fulfil all righteousness.'

The Gospel of Mark begins with Jesus' proclamation: 'This is the time of fulfilment. The Kingdom of God is at hand. Repent and believe in the gospel.'

The Gospel of Luke quotes the child Jesus, who was lost. Mary and Joseph finally find him, and his mother tells Jesus that she and Joseph have been looking for him. Jesus responds to his anxious parents, 'Why were you looking for me? Did you not know that I must be about my father's work?'

The Gospel of John records Jesus' first words addressing two of John's disciples who were following him along the way: 'What are you looking for?' he asked.

These first recorded words of Jesus tell us something about the themes we will see throughout his life: righteousness, the Kingdom of God, repentance, the will of his Father, the call to discipleship.

Even in the first words of Jesus in Scripture we get a sense of who he is and why he has come. We can learn the ways his mission continues through the words he speaks as his life goes on.

At Cana, when the hosts had run out of wine, Mary tells Jesus about their problem. Although he asks Mary what concern that is to him, he says to the servants, 'Fill the jars with water'. We know the miracle that ensues.

Jesus invites people saying, 'Come after me', or similar words. Always Jesus issues an invitation; always he seeks a free response.

Jesus taught with his whole life, and he taught in words. What words touch your heart? He taught the Beatitudes, 'Blessed are the poor in spirit', he said, and with those words began to change the concept of what being blessed means.

He told his followers, 'You are the salt of the earth' and 'You are the light of the world', and so we see what he expects of those who seek to live as he asks. And we see what he knows we can become, the impact that we can have on the world.

Jesus said a lot about external practices that were void of meaning or were done for the approval of others. 'When you give alms,' he said, 'do not blow a trumpet.' And, 'When you fast, groom yourself.'

Jesus taught us to pray. He said, 'This is how you are to pray: "Our Father in heaven …".' He gave us those words to pray, those words we pray each Sunday, and in those words he gave us the attitudes we are to have towards God and neighbour.

What can we tell about this Jesus when he says, 'Where your treasure is, there your heart will be', and bids us put treasure in heaven? What can we learn about him as he declares, 'No one can serve two masters'?

Many times in the Scriptures, Jesus says, 'Do not worry, do not be afraid' as a refrain repeated. He understood human fears; he knew the cost of discipleship would make some followers afraid.

This Jesus challenged his listeners as he spoke, 'Stop judging'. He comforted his listeners when he said, 'Ask and you will receive'. He taught, 'Do unto others as you would have done to you', and throughout his teaching addresses how we are to treat others.

Jesus bids those who would be his disciples to, 'Enter through the narrow gate'. He says these amazing words to the man who was paralysed, 'Rise, pick up your stretcher and go home'. We know from these words and from other words he speaks that Jesus was a miracle-worker.

But he was more than a doer of marvellous deeds. Jesus says, 'Your sins are forgiven', and it caused fury among the people. Only God could forgive sin and here was Jesus forgiving sin! And so we know even from his words that this is the Son of God.

Jesus spoke many words in stories too. He spoke words to tell us what the Kingdom of Heaven is like. It is like a mustard seed that grows far larger than expected and houses the birds. The Kingdom of Heaven is like yeast that leavens the whole of the dough. It is like a buried treasure for which one sells everything in order to purchase. The Kingdom of Heaven is like a pearl of great price; one sells all one has in order to own this pearl.

Sometimes Jesus' words are very clear and to the point. Sometimes his words make one wonder what he was thinking about when he said them. What was he thinking when he said,

'I'm sending you like sheep in the midst of wolves', or when he warned, 'You will be hated by all because of my name'?

How well Jesus, being human like us, understood the human condition. Do you ever wonder what he was feeling when he offered, 'Come to me all you who labour and are burdened and I will give you rest'?

Jesus' words continually call his followers to growth in understanding and in faith. When they experience the storm at sea and finally wake the sleeping Jesus, he says, 'O you of little faith, why did you doubt?' And when some of his disciples want to keep the children from 'bothering' him, he says, 'Let the children come to me'.

Jesus says, 'Ephphatha' (be opened) to the deaf man. And he asks his closest friends, 'Who do people say the Son of Man is?' What was he thinking as he asked that question? Or when he turned then and looked at his followers and asked, 'Who do you say that I am?' Jesus asked a lot of questions and he gave a lot of answers, and his words often turned people's worlds upside down.

Jesus has many instructive words for those who wish to follow him and as we read the words again, we might ask whether we wish to follow him. He says, 'Deny yourself, take up the cross and come.' He says that if we are his disciples, we are to love our enemies, to forgive seventy times seven and to be last if we would be first.

What did Jesus know when he said, 'See that no one deceives you'? And what does it tell us about him when we hear him speak with confidence to his disciples, 'I shall go before you into Galilee'? What was in Jesus' heart as he uttered, 'Do this in memory of me', or as he agonised and prayed, 'Not as I will but as you will'? Do we know the mind and heart of this one who commissioned us to 'go and make disciples'? Do our words match his?

But, if we are to know Jesus Christ, his words are not the whole story. The Scriptures recount the deeds of Jesus and so we come to understand him and to see his mission more clearly. What did he do, this Jesus? Well, even as a young boy, he sat in the temple in the midst of teachers listening to them and asking them questions. We are told that throughout his childhood and youth, Jesus advanced in wisdom and age and grace as he grew.

And then the Scriptures say nothing more of this period in Jesus' life. Years go by and we do not hear what he says and we do not see what he does. What does this silence say? He was obedient to mother and father we're told, but what else can we know of his mind and heart in those hidden years?

What does it say that he stayed out of public? Did he surprise his peers in the schoolyard or amaze people with his carpentry but no one paid attention, no one wrote it down? And then the public years come. What does it say of Jesus' mind and heart in the deeds he did, the life he lived for those three years?

Baptised by John in the Jordan, he was led by the Spirit to the desert. There he fasted and he faced temptations. Then he preached throughout all of Galilee, teaching in their synagogues, proclaiming the gospel of the Kingdom and curing every disease and illness among the people. And, the gospel says, he would withdraw to deserted places to pray.

We read in the Scriptures of the many mighty deeds he performed. He touched Peter's mother-in-law's hand and the fever left her. He drove out evil spirits by a word and cured the sick. He even healed people who were ill or who had disabilities on the Sabbath, and that was a problem for those who made the Sabbath more important than love of God and neighbour. In Nazareth, his native place, he did not work many mighty deeds because of their lack of faith. People's faith was a prerequisite for Jesus' deeds it seems.

What else did he do during the public ministry years? He 'went up on the mountain side by himself to pray' or to the sea or other quiet places. Always he was in loving communication with his Father.

Jesus often surprised his disciples with what he did: the miracles, the inclusiveness of his love and the night 'he came towards them walking on the sea'. What was in his mind and heart when he took Peter, James and John and led them up a high mountain by themselves and was transfigured before them?

One day, he called a child over and placed the child in their midst as an example of discipleship. Another day, he entered the temple area and drove out those engaged in selling and buying there. What was in the mind and heart of this Jesus, what was inside of him as he began to wash the disciples' feet? Is the same stuff in us, in our every deed?

In the Scriptures, Jesus is revealed not only in his words and acts, but through those around him. We learn about Jesus sometimes through what others have to say about him. The prophets had a lot to say – long before he came. Before he was born, the angel Gabriel announced that it was through the power of the Holy Spirit that this child would be conceived. In a dream, an angel spoke to Joseph about the child to be born of Mary and the angel said, 'He will save the people from their sins'.

What did Mary and Joseph say about him to each other through the months of waiting? What did they say about him as they journeyed Bethlehem and when they found there was no room in the inn? Angels at his birth proclaimed to shepherds watching flocks that 'He is a saviour born for you who is Messiah and Lord'.

When Mary and Joseph presented the baby Jesus in the temple, Simeon said of him, 'My eyes have seen God's salvation'. And the prophetess, Anna, as Jesus was presented in the temple 'spoke about the child to all who were waiting the redemption of Jerusalem'. Would she have told us? Or are we waiting for something else?

John declared his cousin, Jesus, 'is mightier than I; I am not worthy to carry his sandals'. A voice from Heaven spoke as Jesus was baptised by John in the Jordan, 'This is my beloved son with whom I am well pleased'.

The leper said to Jesus, 'If you want to you can make me clean' and affirmed Jesus' power to heal. And when Jesus calmed the storm at sea, his disciples questioned, 'What sort of man is this whom even the winds and the sea obey?'

Those who did not follow him had things to say as well. They questioned Jesus and his behaviour: 'Why does your teacher eat with tax collectors and sinners?' They might have worried that they would be expected to do the same.

What does it tell us about who Jesus is as they question: 'Where did this man get such wisdom and mighty deeds? Is he not the carpenter's son?' Herod said of Jesus, 'This man is John the Baptist'. And seeing Jesus walking across the water at night, his disciples said, 'It is a ghost!' and they were very much afraid.

The crowds declared, 'He has done all things well. He makes the deaf hear and the mute speak.' When Jesus healed the paralytic they said, 'We have seen incredible things today! A great prophet has risen in our midst.' But others who saw Jesus' works asked, 'Doesn't your teacher pay the temple tax?'

The heavenly voice on transfiguration day witnessed again to who Jesus is, saying, 'This is my beloved son. Listen to him'. And when Jesus' dear friend Lazarus died, they said, 'See how he loved him!'

The Samaritan woman who met Jesus at the well said, 'Come see a man who told me everything I have done. Could he possibly be the Messiah?' Those who came to meet Jesus at the beckoning of the Samaritan woman said of him, 'We have heard for ourselves and we know that this is truly the saviour of the world.'

The gospels record what he did and said and how frequently those who heard him or saw him were astonished. Am I astonished? Are you? Some people said of Jesus, 'Nothing like this has ever been seen in Israel', and others said, 'He drives out demons by the prince of demons'. They asked themselves – and each other – 'Could this be the son of David?' And his relatives once said, 'He is out of his mind'. Judas said, 'The man I shall kiss is the one.' And other voices declared, 'He has blasphemed. He deserves to die.' And Peter said, 'I do not know the man.'

Pilate spoke, 'I am innocent of this man's blood', and the people chanted, 'His blood be upon us and upon our children!' And the crowd shouted, 'Let him be crucified!' The chief priests, scribes and elders taunted Jesus, saying of him, as he hung on the cross, 'He saved others, let him save himself!'

When Jesus had died, the centurion and the men with him who were keeping watch at the cross said of Jesus, 'Truly this was the Son of God'. Then, on the third day after the crucifixion, as the holy women approached the tomb where Jesus had been laid, an angel announced, 'He is not here. He is risen'. What do you say about Jesus?

One way to learn about a character in literature is through the device of characterisation that explores how others react to the character. What can we learn about Jesus by looking at how those who encountered him reacted to him?

His mother wrapped him in swaddling clothes and laid him in a manger. 'He came unto his own and his own received him not', John's Gospel tells us. The magi followed his star and offered him gifts and homage. At the river, the Spirit of God descended on him like a dove. In the desert, angels came and ministered to him. And the first disciples left their nets and followed him – they left their boats and followed.

Sometimes, reactions to Jesus were not positive: the people in the synagogue rose up, drove him out of town and led him to the brow of the hill, on which their town had been built, to hurl him down head-long.

Even the disciples sometimes did not know how to react to Jesus: 'The disciples returned and were amazed that he was talking with a woman.' And the Pharisees often conspired against Jesus, and one day they 'went out and took counsel against him to put him to death'.

On the other hand, sometimes such large crowds gathered around him that he got in a boat and sat down and the whole crowd stood along the shore to listen to his teaching. When the disciples saw him walking on the sea their reaction was that 'they were terrified'. And, it is written, that after Jesus taught that he would give his body and blood for nourishment, 'Some of his disciples returned to their former way of life and no longer accompanied him'.

When Jesus calmed storms, people reacted to him. They did him homage, saying, 'Truly, you are the Son of God'. And when he taught, they reacted, 'Do you know that the Pharisees took offence when they heard what you said?' The crowds reacted to Jesus too. They were astonished at his teaching for he taught with authority. And the leper's reaction to Jesus was immediate cleansing. Once a whole town came out to meet Jesus, and when they saw him they begged him to leave their district. Would we have begged him to stay?

Many tax collectors and sinners came and sat with Jesus. And once a woman suffering haemorrhages for twelve years came up behind him and just touched the tassel of his cloak and was healed. A sinful woman reacted to him thus: she bathed Jesus' feet with her tears, wiped them with her hair, kissed them and anointed them.

As his ministry went on, the Pharisees' reactions to Jesus grew in hostility towards him and they approached him to test him. A rich young man's reaction to Jesus was that he went away sad for he had many possessions. And we read that all Jesus' adversaries were humiliated by his wisdom.

One of the ten lepers, having realised he had been healed, reacted to Jesus by returning, falling at his feet and thanking him. The mother of Zebedee's sons had a familiar reaction to Jesus, perhaps: she approached him with her sons and did him homage, wishing to ask him for something. I wonder if that is my approach too often.

Another woman reacted to Jesus by coming up to him with an alabaster jar of costly oil and pouring it on his head. And often great crowds reacted to Jesus with great faith. They came to see him, having with them people who were lame, blind, deformed, mute and many others. They placed them at his feet and he cured them. The crowds were amazed when they saw the mute people speaking, the deformed people made whole, the lame people walking, the blind people able to see and they glorified the God of Israel. And all the people were hanging on his words.

When Jesus made his final entry into Jerusalem, the people reacted to his coming. They waved palm branches and shouted 'Hosanna!' But the Pharisees went off and plotted how they might entrap Jesus in speech. They watched him closely and sent agents pretending to be righteous to trap him.

And others reacted when Judas arrived accompanied by a large crowd armed with swords and clubs. Was this the same large crowd who praised him before? 'Hail Rabbi', Judas said, and he kissed Jesus. Then many gave false testimony against him. They laid hands on Jesus and arrested him.

Then the disciples reacted; they left him and fled. The soldiers blindfolded him (this Jesus who cured blindness); they spat in his face (this Jesus whose spittle opened eyes); and they struck him and they mocked and stripped him.

As he hung on the cross, the thief hanging with him reacted to Jesus, and said, 'Jesus, remember me when you come into your kingdom'. And when he died and then returned, risen, the disciples saw him and worshipped, but they doubted. Thomas, who had his doubts answered, reacted to Jesus, proclaiming him, 'My Lord and my God' .

How do we react to this Jesus? Who do we say he is with our lives? The final revelation of any character is when their inner thoughts are exposed and we are told what they feel. There is not much of this device in the gospel stories, but we have a few glimpses into Jesus' mind there.

He knew, we read, what the Pharisees were thinking. He knew his enemies, as we see as the gospels unfold. He knew their malice and he knew their hypocrisy. Jesus knew his disciples. He knew, Scripture says, from the beginning the ones who would not believe and the one who would betray him.

He knew people's thoughts and he realised the intentions of their hearts. And he knew what his disciples wanted to ask him, and he knew when they were impressed with his deeds. Jesus knew when the people were going to come and try to carry him off to make him king.

We get glimpses into Jesus' heart too. At the sight of the crowd we are told his heart was moved with pity for them because they were troubled and abandoned like sheep without a shepherd.

We see his heart as we read that when he heard of John the Baptist's death, he withdrew in a boat to a deserted place by himself. We read that Jesus loved Martha and her sister and Lazarus, and when Lazarus died Jesus became perturbed and deeply troubled and he wept.

When Jesus saw the vast crowd his heart moved with pity for them and he cured their sick. Moved with pity, he touched their eyes. And when Gethsemane was his heart's dwelling he took along Peter and the two sons of Zebedee, and he began to feel sorrow and distress. He saw the city, Jerusalem, and wept over it.

We can know Jesus Christ intimately as we read the Scriptures and as we reflect on all that Jesus said and did and on what others said about him. We can reflect on how people reacted to him: those who chose to be his disciples and those who desired to end his mission and even end his life. Each time we read Scripture – reflect on it, pray with it – we are invited to deepen our love for and discipleship to this Jesus. Each time we say yes to Jesus, we become better able to share his love with our children and others.

When the thoughts of our minds and the desires of our hearts are brought to light, what kind of characters are we? How does what we say and what we do declare who we are as followers of Jesus and as members of the Catholic Church?

There is so much we can learn from the gospels as we deepen our knowledge of Jesus and help others to know him better. Scripture study helps us to understand the time in which the words were written so that we can grasp the implications of Jesus dining with sinners or speaking with women. When we use our imaginations to enter into Scripture, we can walk with Jesus, respond to what he does and hear him speak to us as he proclaims God's plan for all people. When we enter into Scripture in prayerful reflection, our hearts are touched by this living Word of God.

But there is more to knowledge of the faith than the time when Jesus walked this earth. There is the community he left behind and to whom he sent the Holy Spirit. We learn more about Jesus from their efforts to spread his good news and from their witness to all that he taught. Indeed, the apostles taught in his name and shared their knowledge of Jesus and of faith in him.

The early Christians, like us, had their good times and their difficult times. Yet they continued to proclaim Jesus in the face of persecution and even martyrdom. And all those who joined their community added to the understanding of what Jesus and his teachings mean in each day and age. We don't only have Scripture to help us to know Christ, we have Tradition – the living, on-going teaching of the Church.

What the early Church knew about faith was eventually summarised in the Creeds and in doctrinal formulations. The Church wanted to be sure that people knew Jesus and the Father he revealed, the Holy Spirit he sent and his teachings about the way we are to live.

What do you know about your closest friend or your spouse? Do you hold memories of the times you have spent together? Can you recall significant words that you have spoken to each other? If someone asks where your friend was born, or inquires about your spouse's family tree, are you able to answer? No one would say of a loved one, 'Well, she expects me to learn all about her and her family and her life story'. When we love, we are eager to know as much as we can about the beloved.

Knowledge of the faith is not empty facts that we are required to learn; knowledge of the faith is knowledge of our beloved, Jesus Christ, and his teachings. Knowledge of the faith is knowledge of the community that he began and all that community has done in his name throughout the ages. The more our love grows, the more eager we are to deepen our knowledge. And as knowledge and love grow, our hearts are changed and we live differently.

My neighbours have two young daughters who took dance lessons. When the girls were preparing for their dance recitals, they would come to my house and show me their latest steps. On one occasion, the two were ready to perform their dance for me, but the CD player would not work. They decided to go on with the dance anyway, humming the tune themselves as they moved to the music. As they danced, the humming got softer and softer until I could no longer hear the sounds to which they danced. But dance they did, to the music that was inside of them.

This is the point of learning knowledge of the faith: it all becomes the music for our dance of discipleship. It plays inside of our hearts – the words of Jesus, his embrace of the poor and the outcasts of society, his insistent 'Come, follow me'. The music of the Church community and all that holy women and men have done to spread the kingdom of God is the score for our own moving through this world and into the kingdom.

Jesus and his disciples were on the road to Caesarea Philippi when he asked them, 'Who do people say that I am?' The disciples told Jesus that some people were saying he was John the Baptist, others were saying he was Elijah or one of the prophets. Then he asked, 'But who do you say that I am?' And Peter responded, 'You are the Messiah.'

Peter knew Jesus. He had heard him teach, he had watched him heal the sick and embrace public sinners. Peter had walked with Jesus and shared life with him.

We, too, can walk with Jesus, hear his words, watch him, stand beside him as he teaches and cures the leper and heals the blind man and calls us to love. We share life with Jesus Christ. And the question he asked of his disciples as he walked with them is the question he asks us today, 'Who do *you* say that I am?' Not 'Who was I', but 'Who *am* I' for you? Who am I in your decisions, in your relationships, in your words and deeds each day? We answer, not just by professing our faith in Jesus, but by living as he did and as he asked us to live. Returning over and over to the Scriptures in study and prayer and reflection, we gain new insights and are always both comforted by God's love for us and simultaneously challenged to love one another.

Obviously, we cannot live as Jesus did if we don't know how he lived. Knowledge of the faith, loving knowledge, is the foundation for the ongoing life of faith.

For Reflection

Who do you say that Jesus is?

Share a favourite gospel story and what this story tells you about Jesus.

Which of Jesus' teachings do you find most difficult at this point in your life?

Chapter IV

'Ask, and it will be given to you'
(Luke 11:9)

'Keep in touch!' We often enjoin those we love to stay in communication with us, especially when they will be far away, or when we know it will be a long time before we see them again. How do you 'keep in touch' with loved ones?

There are many ways to communicate today which were not available to people who lived before us. We can still write letters and post them – such communication may take days or weeks to reach our loved one, but it is a way to share news and feelings. We can also e-mail or text message, something which arrives instantaneously. We can call on a mobile phone or even 'meet' via internet services. These internet connections provide images as well as voice so they are not only instantaneous, but also relay the nuances of voice and expression, which help us to better understand what our loved one feels and is experiencing.

When we do not see a person and do not communicate in some way, we 'lose touch'. We no longer know what is happening in his or her life, we cannot share each other's joys and sorrows, successes and failures. Others are not aware of our needs or we of theirs. Such disconnection affects our relationship and, if communication is not renewed, can even end a relationship.

Family or school reunions can bring us face to face with people we have not seen or communicated with in years. We may discover that these people – once close friends, perhaps – have gotten married, or had children, or suffered a serious illness, or changed jobs, or had a family member die. Even in reconnecting there is the sense that we have missed too much; it will take years just to catch up with all that each of us has experienced and to grasp the ways that our experiences have shaped us and changed us. We may even leave such a reunion saying, 'Let's stay in touch!'

When we know Jesus Christ and love him, we want to communicate with him. And so we are called to prayer. Throughout history, humankind has sought to communicate with and influence the supernatural powers that they believed to be in charge of the world. Ancient peoples built monuments to these gods and offered sacrifices to express their thanksgiving, to secure the favour of the gods or to appease their wrath. We read about such efforts of humans to communicate with the gods in Greek and Roman mythology. We know, too, that these gods were unmoved by the actions of humans – the gods were too busy with their own concerns and their wars.

The God of the Israelites was so very different. He was the one who initiated the conversation with the people he had created. God revealed himself to his chosen people, spoke to them through the prophets, and they spoke back, sometimes thanking God for the many gifts they had, sometimes grumbling. This God was intimately involved with the people he had chosen. We can hear the conversation between God and his people when we read and reflect on the Old Testament.

Then God spoke the ultimate Word to all humanity: his only Son, Jesus Christ, became a human person. What must it have been like to live when Jesus did? For those who believed he was the Promised One of God, it must have been incredible to actually speak with him; to listen to his teachings; to hear the voice of the Messiah.

And Jesus taught that God wants to hear from us, that God is our loving Father and listens to us. 'Ask, and it will be given to you; search, and you will find; knock, and the door will be opened for you' (Luke 11:9). He tells us, 'Whatever you ask for in prayer with faith, you will receive' (Matthew 21:22). And he assures us, '[I]f you ask anything of the Father in my name, He will give it to you' (John 16:23).

So, how do we ask for, search through and knock at the door of prayer? How do we ask for something, search for what is important and knock on someone's heart-door in the loving relationships of our lives? Communication between people can take many forms and has a variety of purposes. When we speak with someone we love, we may indeed ask that person for something; we may seek their advice or reassurance. We might praise some good that the person has done or a quality the person possesses that we admire. In loving relationships, there comes a time to say, 'I am sorry', and sometimes we turn to someone we love to ask for something for another person, 'Could we help our neighbour in her illness?' We speak words of thanks for the beloved's being and doing. And when we love someone, there is the communion of shared silence as well.

Our communication with God, our prayer, has similar purposes: to express our love, to present petitions, to offer thanks, to praise, to voice sorrow, to make intercession for others.

'Why pray?' I have heard people say, 'God already knows everything'. It reminds me of the spouse who says, 'Why say "I love you" when you already know it?' Expressing our love keeps it alive; saying thanks makes gratitude real; saying we are sorry acknowledges our offence and aids healing; asking something for others keeps us aware of their needs and what we might, with God's grace, do to help. And when we allow ourselves to be silent in God's loving embrace, there is prayer beyond words.

Catholics have a rich heritage of prayer and many ways to pray. There are the prayers we memorise, which become part of our repertoire for praying with the community of faith and foster our sense of belonging. There are the spontaneous prayers, which arise from our hearts and from the situations of joy or sorrow or need in which we find ourselves. We pray powerfully in song.

When we pray and when we teach others to pray we tap into that heritage. When I was a child, I often went to our parish church to pray. There was a shrine of sorts that had a large crucifix above and a kneeler in front of it. Below the crucifix was a prayer encased in plastic, the 'Prayer Before the Crucifix'. I remember some of the words still, having prayed it often. I did not understand all of the words and their meanings, but kneeling there I could feel the faith of all the people who had also knelt and prayed the 'Prayer Before the Crucifix'. Somehow it connected me with the Communion of Saints – those who had gone before and those who prayed the prayer that day or night or the next week. Sometimes we don't need to understand all the words.

Our Catholic heritage holds Scripture as an inspiration for prayer and a source for prayer. We can read a Scripture passage and meditate on the Word of God. The ancient practice of *lectio divina* invites us to prayerfully read Scripture, reflect on it, share our thoughts and live as the Word asks. Scripture drama can engage us in a story and lead us to pray. In our own prayer and in our teaching of prayer we know that listening is a dimension of prayer too.

One of the definitions given for prayer in the dictionary is 'a slight chance', as in, 'You haven't got a prayer of making the team'. There is more than a slight chance our prayers are heard – Jesus has assured us that every prayer is heard – but what about the answer to prayer? Anyone who has prayed mightily for something and that something did not happen may question the power of prayer. Prayer is not a good luck charm, but for the person of faith it does somehow make the unbearable more bearable. Just the belief that we are not alone is a gift of prayer.

It was my father who first taught me a lesson about answers to prayer. I was very young, maybe seven or eight years old. It was early December and I was making my 'wish list' for Christmas gifts. Of all the wonderful things I saw in the colourfully illustrated catalogue, there was one that seemed the most magical to me: it was a globe with an internal light. When you turned the light on in a dark room, the globe projected all of the constellations of stars on the ceiling. That globe was first on my list; it was enormously expensive. When my dad saw my list and spied the globe written at the top of it, he shook his head, but said nothing. That night, he took me by the hand and led me to the windows in my bedroom. 'Look', he said, 'you don't need a globe. All the stars in the sky are yours!' That globe was not under the tree on Christmas morning, but I was not disappointed. I got something better: all the real stars in the sky were mine.

I think prayer is like that; we ask for something and do not perceive that what we ask for is so much less than the blessing we will receive. There are times when we can look back and realise that what we were praying for was not the best thing. We may even say, 'Thank God that didn't happen!' Other times, it is hard to understand; what we asked for still seems best to us. That is why trust is a critical attitude for prayer.

How did the first disciples learn to pray? It is surprising to see how much they experience with Jesus before prayer seemed to become important to them. In Luke's Gospel, Jesus' first disciples were called by him, and, at his direction, they cast out into the deep for a catch even though they had fished all day with no results. They did as Jesus asked and caught so many fish their nets were breaking. They were with Jesus when he cleansed a leprous man and had healed a paralytic man.

Luke's Gospel goes on with the story of Jesus dining with tax collectors and sinners. Then Jesus had taught about fasting and the Sabbath and cured the man with a withered hand. He had taught about loving enemies and not judging others. He had healed the centurion's servant and raised the widow's son from death. Jesus had his feet washed and head anointed by a sinful woman and forgave her sins. Jesus had calmed the storm at sea when the disciples were afraid and asked them to have faith. He healed the Gerasene demoniac, raised Jairus' daughter from death and cured the woman with the haemorrhages.

Then Luke's Gospel recounts how Jesus gave the twelve apostles their mission to proclaim the kingdom of God and to heal. He fed five thousand men (and women and children too, we presume) with five loaves and two fish. He foretold his death and resurrection and was transfigured before Peter, James and John. He healed a boy who had been possessed by a demon and he appointed seventy more disciples to carry on his mission and proclaim the good news of God's love.

Jesus' disciples had witnessed so much! They had lived with Jesus, watched his work and listened to his teachings about God the Father and the kingdom. They saw how he healed and forgave sin.

It is after all of this in Chapter 11 that the Gospel of Luke says:

> He was praying in a certain place, and after he had finished, one of his disciples said to him, 'Lord, teach us to pray, as John taught his disciples.' (Luke 11:1)

Jesus gives his disciples what we now know as the Our Father, the Lord's Prayer. But it is much more than words that Jesus offers, he is also teaching them – and us – the attitudes with which we are to pray. 'Our Father' is recognition that we are all brothers and sisters and have one Father. We are to keep his name holy, honour it in word and deed.

The words of the Our Father remind us that our prayer should be about fostering the growth of his kingdom and being grateful for and satisfied with enough bread (whatever that bread might be) for just this day. We are to forgive others as we want to be forgiven and have the desire to overcome temptations. These are the attitudes of disciples of Jesus Christ.

The words Jesus gave to his disciples are the words we pray at Mass, but the attitudes expressed in these words are part of the prayer as well. When we pray the Our Father, we recognise that all people are our sisters and brothers. We pray for God's name to be kept holy and for his kingdom to come, but we have to be willing to work for these things. We pray for God's will to be done, but we open ourselves to do God's will. We pray for our daily bread but need to be content when the day's needs are fulfilled. We pray that God will forgive us as we forgive others, and in that prayer presumably we embrace forgiveness and forgiving. We ask that we not be led into temptation and that we be preserved from evil, and we are prepared to avoid temptations and with God's grace resist evil. In teaching the Our Father, Jesus was also teaching that we must live what we pray.

What can we learn for our own prayer, and for those whom we teach to pray, from the way Jesus prayed? We might examine the Scriptures to find the answer to this, for he did not only hand down words or even attitudes alone, he gave us a model of prayer showing where he prayed, with whom he prayed, when he prayed and why he prayed.

So where did Jesus pray? One might say, where *didn't* Jesus pray? Jesus was a Jew and so, of course, he prayed in the temple. In fact, the one account we have of Jesus being angry is when the buyers and sellers were making the temple other than a house of prayer.

He prayed in many other places too. Jesus prayed in the desert when he was tempted. What desert times call us to prayer? What temptations can we thwart with prayer? Jesus fasted too, and we might consider this discipline as an aid to prayer sometimes.

Jesus prayed in deserted places. We don't know where these places were, only that no one else was there. Where do we find deserted places to be with God in prayer?

He prayed on the mountain, perhaps again in solitude. Did the majesty of the mountains remind him of his Father? What beauties of creation inspire your prayer? Some people can't physically go up a mountain or stand on the ocean's shore or in a forest of towering trees, so they use a photo or a painting to recall the Father's love and power.

Jesus prayed at his Baptism by John in the Jordan. Nature must have been a special place for him to know his Father's presence. He prayed, scripture recounts, in a 'certain place' (Luke 11:1). Where was it? What was it like? Do you have a 'certain place' for prayer? Do you provide a 'certain place' for others as you teach them to pray?

The upper room was the site of Jesus' prayer the night before he died. It was a borrowed space where he gathered with those he loved to say farewell and to give them an example of how they were to serve and love one another. The places in which we gather with loved ones – around the dinner table, at family celebrations and during family crises – can be the upper rooms of our lives. And the places where we serve others in our families, our neighbourhoods and communities call us to pray to him in whose name we serve.

In the garden of Gethsemane, Jesus prayed as we did not hear him pray before that night. Where are the 'night before' places in which we have prayed – before a decision, before a surgery, before a painful farewell?

And, finally, after a life lived in obedience to his Father, after the sufferings he endured, Jesus prays from his cross. How extraordinary! We might comprehend how someone would pray *before* they experience the cross; we may appreciate that *after* they experience the cross they would pray in thanksgiving that it is over. This Jesus prays *from* the cross – in the throes of dying. Are the crosses in our lives 'places' of prayer even as we bear them? Can we help those we teach that prayer can sustain us even in the midst of hurt and suffering? Jesus also must have prayed when he was on the Sea of Galilee and as he walked along the roads with his disciples to the next town to proclaim the Good News.

With whom did Jesus pray? Often the Scriptures tell us that he prayed alone. He prayed alone sometimes 'with his disciples near him'. There were others around when he prayed before healing people. Did they join the prayer or just stand by? Certainly he tried to pray with his disciples in the garden of Gethsemane; he asked them to pray, but they slept. He prayed anyway. We might grow discouraged when others do not pray, but pray anyway. Scripture does not include every moment of Jesus' life or every time he prayed. He must have learned to pray from his mother and Joseph. Surely he prayed with his dear friends Mary, Martha and Lazarus when he visited with them, and with Nicodemus when he came to Jesus at night. There is so much we do not know for certain about Jesus' praying, but can only imagine.

When did Jesus pray? Scripture includes times of day and night that Jesus turned to his Father and they seem as varied as the places in which he prayed. We even read that he sometimes spent the whole night in prayer. When he taught his disciples to 'pray always' he had shown them what that meant: at all times of day and in all the times of life. Which times move you to pray? When we teach others to pray, do we teach not just morning and night prayers, but also the stop-in-the-middle-of-whatever-you-are-doing kind of prayer that keeps us mindful of God's loving presence?

Time for prayer need not be 'separate' from all that we do to glorify God and serve our neighbour, but intimately woven into our most menial tasks, our most glorious achievements and our most painful losses.

Why did Jesus pray? He prayed to keep in communication with his Father, of course. After all, he was here to do the Father's work and to proclaim the beginning of God's kingdom. When you are doing someone else's bidding, it's important to be in touch with that person.

He prayed before he called the twelve, before he made his decision. He was seeking the Father's guidance, and perhaps asking that those he called might respond with generous hearts. Jesus prayed as he healed people and raised people from death. Scripture tells that he prayed aloud on some of these occasions, to glorify God and offer thanks to him. He prayed to offer blessing: on the loaves and fish; on the children who came to him; on the bread and wine at the Last Supper; on the bread he shared with the disciples on the way to Emmaus. He prayed to cast out demons from those possessed. He prayed for his disciples at the Last Supper. He asked God to protect them, to keep them united to him and to each other. He prayed that they would know joy and be made holy in the truth. Jesus prayed for all those who would believe in him through the preaching of his disciples.

Why do we pray? When we pray for others, do we echo Jesus' prayer to ask for blessings and protection and joy for others? When we teach prayer to our children, do we invite them to be aware of others' needs and not only their own? Jesus prayed for his disciples the night before he died. He could have focused on his own impending death, become absorbed in what he was facing, but instead he prayed for them. He knew it would be hard for them to be without his physical presence.

Prayer can open us to others' needs and in the opening keep us from concentrating only on our own needs. Jesus taught us so much about prayer by his own prayer. How often his prayer began with thanking God and glorifying him. He prayed too, rejoicing in the Holy Spirit. Gratitude, praise and joy were hallmarks of the prayer of Jesus.

In Matthew's Gospel, he teaches us not to pray like the hypocrites, seeking only the attention and admiration of those who see them pray. He bids us to pray alone. He tells us not to 'heap up empty phrases', thinking more words mean more effective prayer! He taught that when we pray we should be ready to forgive and that we should pray for our enemies. He taught us to pray when we face temptation.

What Jesus showed us is that prayer is about our relationship with him and with the Father and the Holy Spirit. Our attitudes mean more than the words we say or the silence we enter into. Prayer is not just something we do, it is a dimension of the loving relationship with God that is our life. That is why in Luke's Gospel we hear Jesus telling a parable about the 'need to pray always and not to lose heart'. We cannot pray always if prayer is simply an add-on to life. Certainly Jesus prayed, but he lived in prayer – all that he did and all that he taught was prayer.

While not replacing certain times to focus on saying prayers, all of our lives can be prayer too. How do we teach our children to 'pray always'?

Recently, the beloved grandfather of friends of mine died. At the funeral Mass, one of the grandchildren led the General Intercessions and began by saying, 'Our prayers today flow from Grampy's influence in our lives'.

Who taught you to pray? Whose example of prayer and a life lived in prayer has influenced your own prayer? How is your prayer and life of prayer influencing others?

There are many people who have taught me to pray. My family certainly taught me prayer. We prayed the family Rosary during October each year; my grandmother's devotion to the Rosary taught me about prayer. Some people were my catechists and taught me prayer. But I continue to learn as I watch people pray through their illnesses and in their joys. In my early life, many prayers I learned were 'me and God' prayers, prayed alone. I have learned to be more comfortable praying with others and having them pray with and for me.

When I was young, there were many community devotions that also influenced my prayer life: processions and Benedictions and Holy Hours and novenas. Some of these are being reclaimed as Catholics see meaning in these forms of prayer, beyond a kind of superstition that said, 'If I do this, God will do that'.

Meditative and contemplative prayer have grown in popularity in our contemporary world. Perhaps the extreme business of life and constant bombardment of media and technological communications has made us appreciate silence. And this is not an empty silence but one permeated with God's presence.

There are many postures for prayer too. We might kneel or stand; we might sit to pray or for night prayer we may be lying in bed. Sometimes we hold hands to pray and sometimes we may adopt a meditative posture as we sit outdoors in God's creation or simply on the floor in our homes.

The place we pray can be anywhere, but sometimes it helps to have a special place where we go alone or with others to speak with God. A simple environment set in our homes and in our classrooms can help us to focus for prayer. We might have a Bible and perhaps a work of art or a beautiful cloth, and we may have a music player that can provide for sung prayer or background music for meditation.

What a gift we have in prayer! And what richness of ways to pray and times to pray we have to share with our children, and our friends, and to expand our own praying always. Through the gift of prayer we are never alone. We are always heard, and when we listen to what God asks we are strengthened to do what he asks. Because we pray and maintain our loving relationship with God, we can do what he asks with joy. Prayer can help us to overcome self-righteousness and the desire to take revenge or to hold a grudge.

'Praying always' turns our most mundane daily tasks and the extraordinary events of our lives into responses to God's love.

The disciples learned well what Jesus had taught. In the *Acts of the Apostles* we read about the followers of Jesus: 'They devoted themselves to the apostles' teaching and fellowship, to the breaking of the bread and the prayers' (Acts 2:42). Our own witness to prayer will be the best lesson we can offer.

For Reflection

Look again at where Jesus prayed, with whom, when and how he spoke with his Father. What way might you try to pray in your own prayer life?

What does it mean to you to 'pray always'? Are there parts of your life you do not see as prayer? What might help you to 'pray always'?

Set an environment for prayer in your home or class. Have family members or students make choices about what will help them to focus on prayer.

Chapter V

'Do this in remembrance of me'
(Luke 22:19)

Our loving relationships with others grow in many ways and our relationship with Jesus grows similarly. We come to know him and all that he did and taught. We speak to him and listen to him in prayer. But always relationships seek to encounter the other – to meet and to celebrate. Jesus is not physically present to us like our other loved ones, of course, yet we have special ways to encounter Jesus through the liturgy and the sacraments.

These special moments echo events in the life of Jesus and his followers and are rooted in those events. Jesus' own Baptism foreshadowed the Baptism we received; Confirmation is the continuing Pentecost as we, like the apostles at the first Pentecost, are sealed with the Gift of the Holy Spirit. We find in the Last Supper the Mass and the Sacrament of the Eucharist as Jesus gives us his own Body and Blood, as he gave himself to his friends the night before he died. The Last Supper is also the root of Holy Orders, and in the wedding celebration at Cana we see Jesus' affirmation of marriage. The Anointing of the Sick is an encounter with Jesus the healer; in the Sacrament of Penance and Reconciliation Jesus forgives sins as he did for people he met when he was on earth.

Some of our sacramental encounters with Jesus Christ may have happened when we were babies or when we were very young children. Think of your early experiences of the Mass. Could you see what was going on or were you buried in the middle of an adult assembly that blocked your view? I know I could not see, although my parents tried to position us up close to the sanctuary. I remember having a pearl-white children's Mass book, which, while most of the text was in Latin back then, also had pictures that I could look at and compare to what was happening at the altar.

Many of our memories of the Mass – certainly our Baptism if we were infants when we received it, and even our First Penance and First Communion – may be dim at best. Some of the memories of these celebrations may even be focused on inconsequential details. What do you remember about your first celebration of the Sacrament of Penance? What do you recall about your First Communion? I remember endless practising for the procession; I remember my father's uncle, who was not Catholic, coming from far away to attend the party afterwards. He brought me a gift: a complete cowgirl outfit, with a pearl-button shirt and cowboy boots. And I remember how upset my parents were when I snuck up to my room, changed from my white dress and veil and reappeared in the new cowgirl clothing. Hardly a sacramental memory!

The *General Directory for Catechesis* names liturgical formation as one of the dimensions for forming disciples. I was asked as a young adult to prepare the children whom I was teaching for the Sacrament of Confirmation. Since I had not thought about Confirmation since I had received it when I was ten, I was quite unsure of what to teach. All I remembered of Confirmation was the red robe and beanie I wore – and I only remembered that because we had a photo.

I had to study, to learn, or learn again, what Confirmation was all about in order to share it. I reflected again on the Scripture story of the first Pentecost and the power of the Holy Spirit in the lives of the apostles. I studied the *Rite of Confirmation* to recall the celebration and the meaning of the symbols in the Rite. I thought about the Holy Spirit's inspiration in my life and the guidance the Spirit offered that so often led me to know and to do what was right. Sometimes remembering, studying and reflecting is what we, as parents and catechists, have to do when we journey with others to their celebration of sacramental encounters. And as we learn in order to teach, we can grow in our understanding of what we celebrated – even if it was long ago.

Remembering events that we experienced can help us and can renew our relationship with those who experienced the event with us. Sharing memories can strengthen our loving relationships and renew our love and commitment to each other. Sharing can help us to recall important details we may have forgotten and even, in some way, make the event live again.

When I changed jobs, I was offered a place to stay with a lovely family while I looked for a place of my own. The mother and father were both in their mid-eighties and had been married for nearly sixty years. After dinner they would tell stories of their first meeting and their courtship. When the story began, they would look at the rest of us as they spoke, but gradually they were caught up in the memory and, as they smiled and spoke and finished each other's sentences, the rest of us ceased to exist. It was like they were back in time, not just remembering the early days of their love, but somehow living those times again.

As we form others for liturgy, telling the stories of our own sacramental moments can help us to grow in love and in our relationship with the Lord. Such sharing can help those we teach to understand that the liturgy – the sacraments and the Mass – are experiences that live on beyond the celebrations.

Scripture often enjoins us to remember all that God has done. Remembering the gift of the Mass and the sacraments and reflecting on all that God has done and continues to do keeps us grateful. In liturgy we remember, and in remembering what we have celebrated in our encounters with the Lord we renew and strengthen our union with him.

Liturgical formation certainly encompasses preparation for participating in the Mass and receiving the sacraments, but it does not end there. In each of these encounters with the Lord we celebrate *something*, and after the sacramental celebration we remember what we have celebrated and we are to live what we have celebrated.

The Church has called the liturgy the 'privileged place for catechesis'. The liturgy itself catechises and forms us in faith precisely because in liturgy we encounter the Christ. That encounter and the ensuing relationship of love is the aim of catechesis. However, being the privileged place implies there are other places where catechesis happens. The informal catechesis offered in the home and the formal catechesis offered in parishes are important as well. In fact, in a time when people have lost some of the sense of meaning of ritual and symbol, these other times for catechesis are critical for an appreciation of liturgy. Catechesis should prepare us for liturgy. It leads us to the threshold of our sacramental encounter with Christ. And catechesis must also come after liturgical celebrations so that there is time to speak of our experience and to reflect on what we are called – and graced – to do.

Our sacramental life begins with the Sacraments of Christian Initiation: Baptism, Confirmation and the Eucharist. Those baptised as adults may clearly recall the celebration and the symbols and their meanings. For those baptised as infants or very young children, the memories are usually dim or nonexistent. However, there are ways we learn about our Baptism from our family. Some families have a custom of celebrating the baptismal anniversaries of their members. These celebrations may include looking at photos or videos and telling stories. The person's baptismal candle may be lighted and the family may even affirm the ways that member has been a light to them and to their faith. This sort of custom can 'give memories' of the sacrament where there were none before.

What do we remember, or what should we remember, and what do we teach our children about Baptism? The *Catechism of the Catholic Church* tells us that Baptism is 'the basis of the whole Christian life, the gateway to life in the Spirit (*vitae spiritualis ianua*), and the door which gives access to the other sacraments' (CCC 1213). Baptism frees us from sin, makes us children of God and members of the Church. In the celebration, we, or our godparents and parents if we are too young, make the baptismal promises and the profession of faith. We are washed in the water of Baptism and baptised in the name of the Father and of the Son and of the Holy Spirit. We are anointed with sacred chrism, signifying the Gift of the Holy Spirit, and incorporated into Christ who is anointed priest, prophet and king.

The white garment symbolises that we have 'put on Christ'. We are given a baptismal candle to signify that in Jesus Christ we are the 'light of the world'.

When the ceremony is over, what does all of this mean for our lives? Parents, godparents and the community all promise to help the child to grow in faith. This means recognising that the family is the 'domestic church' and appreciating the holiness of family life. It means praying together and being a community of love for God, each other and all people.

However, for those of us whose baptismal celebrations were long ago, for those of us who are adults now, what does it all mean? What do we do to live what we have celebrated and help those we teach to live their Baptisms more fully?

What did we celebrate? We celebrated that we are freed from sin. We still live in a world affected by Original Sin; the atmosphere that may encourage selfishness and sin. To live our Baptism we try, with grace, to avoid sin and to say no to the temptations that entice us.

Our Baptism celebrated that we were claimed by the Father, Son and Holy Spirit and made children of God. We live that reality when we speak and act with the dignity that is ours as sons and daughters of God. We are faithful to our Baptism when we make decisions that reflect the Holy Spirit's guidance, Jesus' teaching and the Father's plan for our salvation.

Baptism makes us members of the Catholic Church. When we respect all members of the Church and fulfil our responsibilities to participate in the life of the Church, we embrace our identity as Catholics.

The promises we made or were made for us at Baptism are certainly clear: we are to reject Satan and all the empty promises that evil offers. And we live the beliefs that are professed at Baptism: belief in God the Father, in Jesus Christ, in the Holy Spirit and the Catholic Church. What difference do those beliefs make in our lives, our homes, our workplaces and our neighbourhoods?

Anointing signifies that one is set aside for a special role. Our role is to carry on the mission of Jesus Christ, to proclaim by word and witness the Good News and to evangelise. We live our Baptism as we teach and share our faith, as we encourage those whose faith has grown cold and as we stand for justice at work and peace in our world.

No longer are we clothed in the white garment of our Baptism. What does it mean, then, to 'put on Christ' where we are today, with whom we find ourselves interacting? We can 'put on' Christ's teachings by applying those teachings to each situation we face. We can 'put on' Christ's attitudes of obedience to God and gratitude and faithfulness. Having been baptised, we 'put on Christ' not as one dons a costume, but as the essence of who we are and how we behave in relation to God and to our neighbour.

Jesus said to his followers, 'You are the light of the world' (Matthew 5:13). Long after the initial flame on our baptismal candle has been extinguished we are still to be a light. But our light is to be a reflection of the light of Christ. What light is needed in your community today?

As a child, I lived in a small village that was very historical and had preserved the gaslight lamp posts that served to illuminate the streets. These may have been sufficient at some point in history, but they are no longer adequate. What contemporary issues need the light of Christ and how can that light be shone in a way that people will see and respond to it?

Baptism entitles us to pray the prayer of the children of God, the Our Father. Praying the Our Father each day and at Sunday Mass is living our Baptism.

The Sacrament of Baptism offers much to celebrate and much to live. The way Baptism is celebrated offers so much for us to talk about with our children. Recalling their Baptisms and the meaning of the water and words, the anointing, the white garment and candle can help them to understand their identity as Catholics.

For catechumens, Baptism is immediately followed by Confirmation. For many of us, the order of reception for the other sacraments is different. The order is not the essential point; that we encounter Jesus is.

Confirmation is also a Sacrament of Initiation, although it may be celebrated separately from Baptism and at a later age. The *Catechism of the Catholic Church* tells us that the Sacrament of Confirmation 'perfects baptismal grace' (CCC 1316). Simply said, this means that Confirmation deepens the effects of our Baptism and celebrates our relationship with God, the Holy Spirit.

The intimate connection between Confirmation and Baptism is made clear in the Rite of Confirmation when it is celebrated apart from Baptism. While candidates may choose a new name, they are encouraged to reaffirm the name given to them in Baptism; while they may choose a new sponsor, they are encouraged to choose one of their baptismal godparents.

The celebration of Confirmation includes renewal of the promises made at Baptism, and the anointing with sacred chrism recalls our first anointing at Baptism. In these ways the Church endeavours to emphasise the unity of Baptism and Confirmation.

We first received the Holy Spirit in Baptism, and in Confirmation the celebrant extends his hands over those to be confirmed and prays for the outpouring of the Holy Spirit on them. Then the minister of the sacrament (usually a bishop) anoints us, lays his hand on each person to be confirmed, and says, 'Be sealed with the Gift of the Holy Spirit'.

Do you recall the celebration of your Confirmation? What name did you choose and who was your sponsor? What, if anything, do you remember? What do you want your children, the children you teach, to remember after the celebration is over? Reflecting on what is really important about the sacrament can help us to live our own Confirmation and to better prepare those we teach.

When Confirmation is celebrated separately from Baptism, the preparation differs depending on the age and maturity of the candidates. In Confirmation, we, in effect, celebrate a new relationship with Jesus Christ and with the Holy Spirit.

It reminds me of how we incorporate a new child into our family. We do not expect the new baby we welcome to do chores and contribute to family discussions. The baby is welcomed as a baby, who brings joy, is cared for, fed, changed and included in family gatherings with no expectations – other than perhaps a smile or a giggle!

As the child grows, more is expected. At an appropriate time, we begin to teach the child how to participate more fully: to converse, to be kind, to help with tasks. By the time the child is a youth, a smile or giggle is pleasant, but it is no longer a sufficient contribution to family life. The youth now is not only to be cared for – which still happens, of course, albeit in different ways – he or she is also expected to show care for others. Gradually, we all move in our development from being a receiver only to being a giver as well.

In infant Baptism, we welcome babies on their own terms. They are gifted with baptismal graces and share in God's life. As members of the Church, the newly baptised babies are not expected to join committees or volunteer for fundraisers or participate fully at Mass. Yet, they are members and, as they bring joy to their families, they are a joy for the Church community as well. We give them the love and care they deserve as children of God.

However, as in a family, we expect that members will grow from being receivers to being givers, so the Church expects the same. As children grow in age, we anticipate their increased participation. Obviously, we teach them what that means, and hopefully our own example teaches too.

Confirmation preparation can help young people to 'try on' the life of the confirmed Catholic. Through prayer and service and participation in liturgy, they practise being committed to living as more than mere recipients of all that Jesus offers through his Church. They practise assuming greater responsibility for his mission. Of course, they have been growing towards this all along and the immediate preparation only emphasises this as they move towards greater maturity.

In the celebration of Confirmation, we are sealed with the Gift of the Holy Spirit. But what does this mean? The *Catechism* says that the effect of the sacrament is 'the special outpouring of the Holy Spirit as once granted to the apostles on the day of Pentecost' (CCC 1302). Will we be changed as they were?

You remember the story I am sure. Jesus had been crucified. The disciples were afraid – not only because they were without Jesus, but they feared for their own lives. They were gathered together, perhaps comforting each other, perhaps encouraging each other to not lose faith. I picture them telling the stories of Jesus. First they would have shared what they experienced during Jesus' suffering and death. And then, maybe, they thought of his life and started to share favourite memories: 'Remember when he cured the deaf man?' or, 'Will you ever forget the time he walked across the sea to be with us?'

Then, as we read in the Acts of the Apostles, 'And suddenly from heaven there came a sound like the rush of a violent wind'. Of course, we know from our perspective that the sound was a sign of the Holy Spirit's coming; they didn't know that. Can you imagine them, gathered in fear, and then a violent sound rushes in? Were they more afraid then?

Then the tongues of fire appeared and rested on each one of them. Did that allay their fears or only increase them? The Spirit's presence may not be immediately comforting.

I sometimes wonder if fear, or at least uncertainty, is the very threshold across which the Spirit enters. It is not at times when I am confident that I know the Spirit's presence; I am self-confident in those times and fail to perceive my need for the Spirit's help. Rather, it is when I am uncertain of what to do, or not sure that I can do what is asked of me, that I turn to the Holy Spirit. And because of Baptism and the outpouring of the Spirit at Confirmation, we are assured that in such times the Spirit responds.

To live our Confirmation, because it is the perfection of baptismal grace, we live it as we live our Baptism. And we embrace the gifts of the Holy Spirit, which were increased in us through this sacrament. We can deepen our use of these gifts and help our children to live them as we share what the gifts help us to do. Through wisdom and understanding we grow in our ability to comprehend what Jesus taught. Right judgement enables us to make decisions consistent with our faith and courage strengthens us to live by those decisions. The gift of knowledge helps us to always seek the truth and to recognise it. Reverence is expressed in our lives as we honour God and show respect for the Divine spark which dwells in every person. When we see all that God has created and remember all that God has done, we live the gift of Wonder and Awe. What story would you tell to someone about to be confirmed about the gift of the Holy Spirit in your life?

My experiences of the Holy Spirit's presence are many and varied. There are the times when I am angry with someone and the Spirit seems to whisper, 'Forgive'. When I see someone in need and am wrapped up in my own concerns, the Spirit simply reminds me to offer help. As a public speaker, I turn to the Holy Spirit before I speak and ask that I might say something that will touch people's faith. On many occasions, a person will approach me after I have given a presentation and say, 'When you said ...' The person will go on to quote words that I am convinced I never said, but somehow the person heard those words and the words made a difference.

The Eucharist is the third Sacrament of Christian Initiation. Those who receive these sacraments at the Easter Vigil join the community at the table of the Eucharist after they are confirmed. For those baptised as infants, the order of reception may be different. For all of us, both Baptism and Confirmation lead us to the Eucharist, which completes our initiation into the Church.

It is impossible to speak of the Sacrament of the Eucharist without also talking about the Mass, the celebration of the Eucharist. The Eucharist is 'the source and summit of the Christian life' (*Lumen Gentium* 11). Everything that the Church does comes from Jesus Christ, who gives himself for us. And all that we do we offer back to him as we gather for the Eucharist each Sunday.

The preparation for participation in the Mass and for the reception of First Holy Communion begins long before celebration. It begins in loving homes where we gather with family and friends, where we tell the stories that remind us of who we are and what our heritage is, and where we are nourished by the food we share, the blessings we offer and the gift of each other. All of this is the holiness of family life, the domestic church that leads us to the holiness of the larger Church and the celebration of the Eucharist.

An image of this reality struck me as I participated in Mass one Sunday. The couple in the pew in front of me had a child who was about two years old. The child behaved well for one so small, but as the Mass went on, he became tired and a bit noisy. As the moment of consecration drew closer, the mother sat the child on the back of the pew in front of her. Mom had brought some sort of tiny snack food along. As the priest elevated the host, the mother held the snack up to her son. My view of all this was: mother, snack, child, host, priest. It was beautiful. What I was seeing vividly captured for me in that instant the role of the family in faith formation and preparation for sacraments. That child will one day be able to understand what the Eucharist is about because he has been lovingly nourished by his family, not just with a snack at Mass, but in all the ways a family nourishes us.

Perhaps he will better understand the many ways of being 'fed' and that the Mass includes all these ways: our stories and heritage as Catholics, the presence of the community that supports us and the Bread of Life, which is Communion.

At the celebration of the Eucharist each Sunday, we gather with the community of faith. We are nourished by God's Word, by the Body and Blood of Jesus Christ in Communion and by one another's love and encouragement. Even before we receive our First Communion, we are being formed by the Word and the community of faith.

At Mass we listen to God's Word and reflect on it and what it says to our hearts and lives. I noticed as my mother grew older that her storytelling changed. Whereas she used to simply tell her stories and the stories of our family, some new dimensions appeared as she aged. First, I noticed that she would begin to tell me a story and then say, 'I told you this before, didn't I?' Even when I responded, 'Yes, you have told it before', she would continue telling it anyway. Sometimes she would begin telling a family story and then abruptly say, 'You finish it'. She would sit back then and simply correct any errors I made in names or dates. At times my brothers and I would be with her and there would be others there as well. Suddenly she would turn to one of us and command, 'Tell the story about Christmas 1971'. When one of us took up the challenge, she again assumed the role of editor, making sure we got every detail correct.

I realised that Mom knew she did not have much time left to tell the stories. Mom was exercising quality control over the stories of our family; she wanted to be sure we knew them and that we could tell them – correctly and completely and faithfully – to the next generation.

Every Sunday Mother Church gathers us and tells us the stories of our faith over and over. Those stories – the Scriptures – are ours to nourish us and to hand on to our children. Mother Church wants to be sure that we know the stories and to be certain that we can hear their echo in our own lives.

We are nourished with God's Word and then we are nourished with the Eucharist. Preparation for the reception of this sacrament, whether for the first time or the thousandth time, begins with recognising the hungers of our hearts and our spirits and our need to be nourished.

Having recognised our hungers, we then need to know that the Eucharist is Jesus Christ, who gives himself to us to be our food. And we need to know that, as regular food changes our bodies, so when we receive the Bread of Life – Jesus Christ – he changes us. As the saying goes, 'You are what you eat'. We are nourished with the Body and Blood of Christ so that we might be transformed by him and be, together, the Body of Christ in and for the world today.

When I volunteered at Misericordia, a home for mentally and physically disabled children, I saw what it means to be 'ready' for Communion. Mark, one of the residents, was about twelve, though developmentally much younger. We were all at Mass together and Mark was in his wheelchair, one that held his head in position, since he had no muscle control.

When communion time came, Mark opened his mouth, and moved his tongue around as one might do when seeing food after a long fast. His whole countenance spoke desire to be fed by the Lord. That is readiness for communion.

The liturgy changes us. At Mass one Sunday, a mom and dad arrived with their toddler daughter. Obviously there had been some problem at home because the couple walked far apart and sat at opposite ends of the pew.

During Mass, the little girl went from one parent to the other, spending time with each. Slowly the man and woman softened their positions, moving closer to each other when they sat again after standing or kneeling. At the exchange of peace, they turned and embraced each other – with their little girl caught up in the middle. Liturgy calls us to change; it does not always happen so immediately, but we are to live what we have celebrated.

When the Eucharistic liturgy is ending, the priest or deacon says, 'Go in peace to love and serve the Lord'. We have been nourished, not so we feel satisfied and full; we are nourished for mission. There is great clarity here about what it means to live the sacrament we have celebrated.

In the movie *The Neverending Story*, the boy, Bastian, reads a book and in the reading he becomes the hero of the story in the land of Fantasia. When he returns to his real life, Bastian is able to solve his problems with the insights he gained in Fantasia. He revisits the bookseller, Mr Coreander, who explains that there are some people who never go to Fantasia and others who go and never return. But there are people, like Bastian, who go to Fantasia and return and they make both worlds better. In liturgy, we imagine what the world could be like if we lived the gospel; we go forth from liturgy to live what we have imagined.

As we try to live as the gospel requires, we will sometimes fail and there will be need for forgiveness and healing. Usually the first Sacrament of Healing we celebrate is Penance and Reconciliation. When I was a Parish Director of Religious Education, I invited the parents of children who were going to receive the Sacrament of Penance for the first time to a gathering. As we began the meeting, I spoke with them about the wonder of God's mercy.

They smiled. I spoke about God's unconditional love and his forgiveness. They nodded and smiled. 'Isn't it incredible that no matter what we have done, God will forgive us?' I exclaimed and they smiled broadly. 'So,' I went on, 'I couldn't think of a better way to begin this evening than by having us all go to confession.'

Their smiles faded; their heads did not nod in agreement. Some looked afraid, some looked sad, others looked angry.

I then told them that we were not really going to go to confession, but that we needed to talk about what they thought and felt when they believed I was being serious. Sometimes people had unpleasant experiences of confession and when that is the case it is important to talk about it so that we might authentically present the gift of reconciliation to our children, youth and adults, and perhaps reclaim it for ourselves.

Reconciliation was Jesus' ministry. He came to reconcile all people to the Father. He often taught about forgiveness: the story of the prodigal son; the parable of the unforgiving servant; the Our Father. And he forgave sin: the woman caught in adultery; the paralysed man; and, perhaps most powerfully, he forgave those who crucified him even as he hung on the cross. He asked that our forgiving be limitless – that we should forgive seventy-seven times. As his disciples, we are to carry on Jesus' ministry of reconciliation, and therefore we have to be people who know forgiveness and forgiving, and what it takes to mend relationships.

As we celebrate the Sacrament of Penance, we are sorry and we confess our sins to one who is human like us, yet forgives in God's name. We do penance to help in the healing of our own woundedness and the healing of our relationship with God and with our neighbour. A priest, who is as compassionate as Jesus was and who can offer guidance as we seek to live more fully as Jesus' disciples, can help us to see this sacrament as a gift.

We begin preparing our children for this sacrament as we teach them about right and wrong. Even before they understand what sin is, we teach them to say 'I'm sorry' when they have hurt someone or done something wrong. We teach them to admit they have done wrong, to be sorry for what they have done and to do what they can to express their sorrow and make up for any hurt they have caused.

We also give an example when we forgive and when we say we are sorry to those we have hurt or when we do something wrong. We are human; we will fail sometimes; our children will fail sometimes. That is why conversion is life-long. Our relationship with Jesus Christ is not based on perfection, but on love. As we experience his forgiveness, that love can grow, and we become more attentive to the graces that help us respond to the God who first loved us. And that is the way we live out what we have celebrated in Penance.

The other Sacrament of Healing is the Anointing of the Sick. We know the stories of Jesus the Healer. He healed bodies and spirits. When members of the Church are seriously ill or in danger of death from sickness or old age, the community of faith surrounds them with prayer. Sometimes the Anointing of the Sick is celebrated at Mass and the community is physically present to give comfort and support. At other times, a priest, along with the family and friends of the person being anointed, represent the whole community for the celebration. Even when it is only the priest and the person being anointed, the community of faith is present through the priest and he gives witness to their prayer and concern.

As we share the meaning of this sacrament with our children, and prepare those who may receive this anointing, we can point to Jesus the Healer and to all of the ways that families can assist their loved ones who are ill.

When someone is very ill, we can encourage them, not by denying their pain or its seriousness, but simply by being with them. And that 'being with' means they are not alone in their suffering. We journey with those who are ill, wherever that journey may lead.

Once I was afflicted with salmonella. I was hospitalised for a week and was extremely ill before they made a diagnosis. I was in isolation; when visitors came, they had to be robed and masked and wear rubber gloves. When I came home, still ill, but now medicated, my pastor invited me to receive the Anointing of the Sick at a parish celebration. That evening, through his sacramental touch, I felt 'touchable' again and knew what the lepers must have felt with Jesus' hand upon them. And I feel that touch anew every time I hear the gospel story of the lepers.

Each time we include our children in our visits to those who are ill or infirm or elderly, we teach them to offer these gifts of presence and compassion. And the Anointing of the Sick then deepens the meaning of what we alone can bring. In this sacrament, the Holy Spirit brings consolation and the grace of strength and courage. The sick person is not alone, because those who love that person are there and because Jesus Christ is with them in their suffering. The sacrament reminds those who are ill that their lives are gift and that their witness in suffering as well as in health builds up the Body of Christ.

In the celebration of this sacrament, the priest anoints the person with blessed oil on the forehead and hands and prays, 'May the Lord who frees you from sin save you and raise you up'. Those who receive this sacrament live what they have celebrated by following Jesus Christ, whether they return to health or they join him in the kingdom of God.

The Sacraments at the Service of Communion are Matrimony and Holy Orders. How do we prepare our children to celebrate and to live these sacraments? How do we live the Sacraments at the Service of Communion that we have celebrated?

Unlike the other five sacraments, what we teach our children about Matrimony and Holy Orders is not for the children's immediate preparation for these sacraments. But all that we do to form them in faith is remote preparation for their eventual reception of or appreciation for the lives of commitment that these sacraments celebrate.

The first school of marriage preparation is one's own family. We, as parents, teach our children what marriage is by the way we live our own marriage. The examples that husbands and wives offer to their children – examples of love, faithfulness, forgiveness, gentleness and selflessness – are the ultimate teaching. No marriage is perfect, of course, and it is important that children learn that as well; no search for the perfect mate will be successful and no marriage will live up to the romantic ideal.

We help our children to learn to express themselves in relationships, to form healthy friendships in which both people grow. We can show them how people can disagree without compromising their own or the other person's dignity. All that we help them to be in relation to family and friends and neighbours prepares them for the Sacrament of Matrimony.

Of course, all that we share with our children about forming good and healthy relationships can prepare them for Holy Orders as well. Whether a man serves as a deacon, priest or bishop, the care of the People of God is his responsibility. He acts in the name of Christ who 'came not to be served but to serve' (Matthew 20:28). Those who are ordained speak God's Word to people and lead God's people in worship and service to others. Those who respond to God's call to Holy Orders must have a tremendous love and understanding of Jesus and of the people they shepherd in order to commit their lives to such service.

Living these Sacraments of Service, for those who have received them, requires faithfulness and generosity. We 'live' these sacraments as a community of faith when we offer support and prayers for married couples, deacons, priest and bishops. As we teach our children about the Sacraments of Service, we invite them to consider the particular vocation to which God may be calling them, whether that be marriage or single life, religious life or ordained ministry.

Celebrating the liturgy helps us to develop our 'sacramental vision' through which we see the presence of God in our world and, most of all, in one another.

The *Catechism of the Catholic Church* refers to the 'symphony of faith'. I think of the liturgy as a symphony in which through story, music, gestures and symbols we express our beliefs and worship our God. The liturgical formation which catechesis offers helps us to participate in that symphony. And we are able to hear its strains and its stories echo in our everyday lives.

I participated in an archaeological dig in Mallorca, Spain. As we dug, we found things – a shard of pottery, a bead, a piece of glass – and the archaeologist would gather us together. He would hold up the 'find' and tell a story about it. I found a bead: was it important or just junk? When the archaeologist told the story of the bead – that it would have belonged to a member of the Beaker people who settled on the island thousands of years ago – it became a treasure.

Every day people 'dig up' things in their lives – a new relationship, an illness, a loss, a joy – and they hold it in their hands. They share it with us wondering what it means. Is it important or is it junk? They look for the story of faith that will help them to understand the meaning of what they have found. The stories of faith that we heard and learned and celebrated in liturgy can give meaning to all that we 'find' in life.

Through the Church's liturgical year she tells the stories of Jesus' Paschal Mystery: his life, sufferings, death and resurrection. The *Catechism* says, 'Christian liturgy not only recalls the events that saved us but actualises them, makes them present' (CCC 1104). There are many ways to live, and help our children live, the liturgical year. A prayer space in the home or class can reflect each season as it is celebrated. Using the colour of the season and some appropriate symbol helps us to recall the particular events of Jesus' life that we are focusing on. As we pray at home or in class we can have a special remembrance of a feast day, or we can tell the story of a saint whom the Church is celebrating. We remember Jesus' story, we remember Mary's story and the other saints' stories and these call forth our own stories into the story of life, death and resurrection in which we share.

Our participation and our children's engagement in the Sunday liturgy can be enhanced when we take time before Sunday to read the Scripture stories that will be used. We might talk about what the stories say to our lives as a family. After Mass, a discussion of the homily can help us to incorporate the lessons through the week.

I remember always feeling as though my life was in the wrong liturgical season. The Church was celebrating the Advent season and I felt like Lent. The liturgical season called for penance and I was rejoicing. It took me many years to realise that the liturgical seasons were calling me beyond my own life events into the bigger events of our faith. Even if I felt a different season in my life, I was called to remember my participation in the Paschal Mystery.

For Reflection

Share a memory of a sacramental encounter with Jesus.

What do you want your children to remember after their first reception of the Eucharist and Penance? How will the preparation for these sacraments focus on what's important?

Consider what you have celebrated in one of the sacraments. What might you do to live that sacrament more fully?

Chapter VI

'Love one another as I have loved you' (John 15:12)

When we have grown to love someone and to communicate with that person and to celebrate together as that love grows, that love changes us and we are different. The love we have for Jesus Christ, our knowledge of him, our prayer to him and our encounters with him in liturgical celebrations change us – and we live differently.

The new life we began with Christ through Baptism is lived by following him in our thoughts, words and actions. We learn how to live and teach others to live as Jesus taught through the dimension of catechesis called 'moral formation'.

The *General Directory for Catechesis* says, 'The Christian faith is above all conversion to Jesus Christ ... a decision to walk in his footsteps; a personal encounter making of oneself a disciple of him. This demands a permanent commitment to think like him, to judge like him, and to live as he lived' (GDC 53).

Living as Jesus asks begins with embracing a positive vision of who we are. We know from the Scriptures and from all that the

Church teaches who we are:

- We are created in the image and likeness of God and are God's children.
- We are redeemed by God's only Son, Jesus Christ, our brother.
- We are temples of the Holy Spirit.
- We are embraced by a community of faith and surrounded and supported by a communion of saints.

Therefore, there are some things that we do and some things that we do not do. Some thoughts, words and actions are consistent with our God-given dignity and some are not. Some thoughts, words and actions respect the dignity of other people, and others do not.

As parents and teachers, I believe we have a positive vision of who our children are and who they are called to be. When asked what sort of people we want our children to be, we may well express those hopes in positive terms. We want them to be loving, generous and kind.

Our positive hopes may not be what we express when two children are quarrelling. 'Don't fight!' we may exclaim, or, 'Stop arguing'. In the immediacy of the moment, we may fail to say, 'I want you to be understanding of each other'. Moral formation includes both the positive aspects of what we are to do as well as the 'do not dos'.

How did your own parents express their hopes for the sort of person you would be? How did they teach you about right and wrong? In moral formation, as in all other areas of catechesis, the witness we give through living as disciples of Jesus Christ is indispensable.

The Ten Commandments are one of the foundations of Christian morality. Just as those laws guided the Israelites, they are also meant to guide us. As we teach our children the commandments, it is important that they know how each commandment tells us what to do as well as what not to do. There are positive ways to live each commandment; there are things that each commandment forbids.

The first three commandments are focused on our relationship with God, the other seven address our relationship with our neighbour. The first commandment requires that we hold to the gift of faith we have been given. We are to nourish our belief in God and to worship him. Nothing in life is to be more important to us than God; we are not to displace him by making possessions or relationships or work or anything else more important in our lives than he is.

Perhaps no one recognises the 'false idols' that we may have more quickly than children do. Children seem to see clearly when something is important to us – and when something or someone is *most* important. And they are quick to imitate us. As your children look at you and your life, what evidence is there that God comes first? How do you help them to keep God as the most important thing in their lives?

The second commandment calls us to use God's name with respect. Respecting a person's name shows respect for that person. We recognise that God's name is holy and that God is holy and deserves our respect.

A friend of mine has a very young nephew. Recently, when she was visiting that little boy and his family, the boy dropped something and exclaimed, 'O, God!' His mother quickly corrected the boy saying, 'You don't say "God" that way'. The little boy responded by making the sign of the cross and saying, 'You can say "O, God" if you do this'.

Perhaps of all the ways we see children imitating us, none is more frequent than their imitation of the language we use. Our respectful use of God's name in prayer and in sharing our faith will be imitated, and so will any misuse.

In the *Catechism* we read another dimension of the second commandment. It says, 'God calls each one by name. Everyone's name is sacred. The name is the icon of the person. It demands respect as a sign of the dignity of the one who bears it' (CCC 2158). We are to show respect for God's name and for other people's names. After all, we are all God's children and who wants the name of their child disrespected? We share the name 'Christian' and that name also deserves respect, as it identifies followers of God's Son, Jesus Christ.

The third commandment reminds us that we are to keep the Lord's Day and holy days of obligation holy. Our participation in the Sunday celebration of Mass is the primary way we keep the Lord's Day holy. It is also a way we express that God is most important in our lives. Many people know the nourishment that liturgy offers in word and sacrament and the presence of the community, and they no longer think in terms of Sunday Mass as an 'obligation'. They realise that it is difficult to live as Jesus' disciples without the encouragement of the Scriptures, the gift of communion and the encouragement of a community of faith.

There are other ways to keep Sunday holy beyond participating in Mass. Sunday is to be a day for rest from work when family can spend time together and deepen their love for and enjoyment of each other. Sunday is also kept holy as we engage in 'good works and humble service of the sick, the infirm and the elderly' (CCC 2186).

There are people whose circumstances require them to work on Sundays and we hold them in prayer as we gather for the celebration of the Eucharist. Often parishes send people from Sunday Mass to visit and bring communion to those who are ill or too frail to attend Mass and to the caregivers who must remain with them.

How do we keep Sunday holy? How do we teach our children all of the ways that we can celebrate the Lord's Day through worship and good deeds and play?

The fourth commandment tells us to honour our father and our mother. This commandment is addressed to children, but it is addressed to adults as well. As people live longer lives, many adults have parents who are still living as the adult children reach middle age and beyond.

It is easy, perhaps, to teach our children to be obedient and respectful to their parents. But how do they see their parents caring for their grandparents? Do they witness patience and care, or benign neglect, or worse? How do they see elders included and accommodated for in the parish? As our elders lose their hearing or ability to walk unassisted, do we provide ways for them to still be able to take part in family events and parish gatherings?

The fourth commandment does not apply only to parents and grandparents: 'It requires duties of pupils to teachers, employees to employers, subordinates to leaders, citizens to their country' (CCC 2199). This presumes that the people in those positions of authority are fulfilling their roles with justice and respect as well.

What do children hear us say about our bosses or our leaders? There may be honest and necessary critiques of behaviour and decisions, but do we show the respect we want our children to have towards authority figures in their own life?

___

The fifth commandment is stated in the negative: do not kill. But the positive requirements of this commandment go far beyond the avoidance of killing. It calls us to respect all life and to protect it from conception to natural death. As we teach our children to respect life, it is important that we include the whole spectrum of life.

When I taught young adolescents, we had a discussion about respecting life. I sensed they were missing something and so had them work in groups on an imaginary scenario. The scenario was that there was not enough oxygen for all the people who were living, so some of them had to be eliminated – killed off. The groups had to decide which people to eliminate. To my surprise, they entered into the task willingly and, to my greater surprise, actually made their elimination lists. The lists included the elderly (they already had long lives), the handicapped (they were not 'productive'), the mentally ill (they could 'cause trouble'). Babies were never listed, nor were children. I realised that what they respected was not all life, but only young and healthy life. Then I told the class that I had also made a list. I had decided to eliminate all brown-haired adolescent students. After their strenuous objections, we talked about God being in charge of life and death. When that authority is taken away from God, it becomes dangerously arbitrary. Do our children learn to respect all life from us?

Respect for life includes caring for our own life and health and that of others. Young people may be tempted to engage in risky behaviour that threatens their health and their very lives; this commandment reminds us that our lives belong to God. This commandment also includes not hurting other people's lives by giving bad example.

In all of these areas, again, it is our witness that speaks most clearly about our beliefs. The fifth commandment requires us to be peacemakers – personally, locally and globally. We help our children work for peace by beginning with their interactions with siblings and peers. They can learn the necessary skills for peacemaking when we model peaceful ways to handle disagreements and conflicts.

The sixth commandment is certainly calling married couples to fidelity. In following the sixth commandment, we are all to respect the holiness of matrimony and to support married couples in their faithfulness to each other.

This commandment calls us all to the virtue of chastity – the integration of our sexuality in loving, healthy and appropriate relationships. We relate to people in physical ways and we know the strength of a handshake, the warmth of a hug. Our bodies are meant to express love in family relationships and in friendships.

In our families and extended families we learn how to express love in many ways. As our children become more mature, we teach them that the marriage act is authentic only in the context of the covenant of matrimony. And they will see how children are welcomed as blessings from God as we embrace them in our families and in the community of faith.

There are couples whose marriages have ended, and these people need the support of their faith community, which embraces them without judgement. Our children will learn this through our example.

The seventh commandment requires that we respect the property of others. But it asks more than merely not stealing or damaging another's property. Our children face temptations to the seventh commandment that generations before did not dream of. There are songs that can be downloaded on 'pirate' sites – much cheaper than actually buying the music. The same goes for computer software, which can also be copied. We can 'steal' another's reputation by posting hurtful information on the internet or by spreading rumours.

The seventh commandment also calls us to justice and charity in dealing with the goods of this world, and it calls us to care for the goods of creation. Do our children see us making an effort to conserve energy and to recycle? Do we explain that we do these things not just to save money but as a way of respecting the resources of God's creation?

The eighth commandment requires that we tell the truth. As disciples of Jesus, we witness to him, who is truth, and to the truth of his teachings. Certainly we teach our children about telling the truth and when they see us telling the truth to our own parents, to our colleagues or to our civic leaders, they learn the value of this.

Even children know that telling the truth is not always easy; they will learn from watching you tell the truth and from their own experiences of admitting the truth. But, ultimately, it is only the truth that sets us free – of anxiety, guilt and regret.

The ninth and tenth commandments ask us to be happy for our neighbours. We should rejoice for them that their marriages are good and that they have possessions that bring them comfort and joy. The trick is to rejoice for them even though we may not have these relationships or possessions ourselves.

Do we celebrate our neighbours' good fortune? Do we teach our children to celebrate with the friends who get something that our children want but can't have? Do we avoid 'keeping up with the Joneses' – buying beyond our means in order to have what others have?

In the Gospel of Mark, we read the story of the rich man who approached Jesus and said, 'Good Teacher, what must I do to inherit eternal life?' Jesus replies, 'You know the commandments' (Mark 10:17-18). The man assures Jesus that he has kept the commandments since he was young.

Then Jesus tells the man that he lacks one thing and invites him to sell what he has and give the proceeds to the poor and then follow him.

The rich man was 'shocked and went away grieving', and we do not know if he ever returned to follow Jesus. Clearly Jesus was teaching us that while the commandments are important, there is more to discipleship.

Later in Mark's Gospel, we read that one of the scribes asked Jesus which of the commandments is the first – the most important of all. Jesus responds that the first commandment is to love God. He does not end his response there, but immediately goes on to say that the second commandment is to love your neighbour as yourself.

The Ten Commandments spell out some of what it means to love God and to love our neighbour. But expressing love for God and neighbour is the purpose of the commandments. How sad that sometimes the commandments are used as weapons to attack those who fall short of their requirements. Do we teach our children that love of God and neighbour are the most important commandments? Can we, in our lives and in our teaching, hold up to the ideals of living the way the Ten Commandments call us to, without falling into the trap of self-righteousness?

When we reflect on Jesus' words, 'love your neighbour as yourself', we may see those words as not just a commandment, but a statement of fact as well. I can see in myself and in others, that, in fact, our love for ourselves is the foundation of our ability to love our neighbours. If we do not love ourselves, we will not take care of ourselves; if I find myself unlovable, it is likely I will find my neighbour unlovable too.

As parents and teachers we play such an important role in loving and affirming our children. How can a child who has not first experienced love go on to love God and neighbour? Moral formation in catechesis is learning to live in love; such formation must be offered, then, in an environment of loving relationships.

All of Jesus' teachings help us to understand the ways to live in love for God and neighbour. The people who followed Jesus and heard his teachings most likely knew the Ten Commandments. Yet, there were societal and even religious practices that were contrary to love. Jesus challenged many of these practices and perhaps did so most powerfully in the Sermon on the Mount as he taught the Beatitudes (Matthew 5:1-12).

In Jesus' time, the Beatitudes must have shocked some people. After all, some of them saw poverty, illness and loss as punishments from God. I doubt that anyone understood persecution as a blessing. We are much more enlightened now though, aren't we? Until we remember that there were people who said the disease AIDS was punishment from God.

Perhaps the Beatitudes are just as shocking today as they were in Jesus' time. Perhaps our understanding of blessedness is still equated with health and wealth and position. Even if we do understand that being poor in spirit and mourning and mercy are blessings, the reward seems distant. I saw a sign recently that said, 'Instant gratification takes too long'. Are we content with delayed rewards? Do we help our children hold off on the cheap 'instant fix' and work towards that which is more lasting?

If we embrace the teachings of the Beatitudes, then as a community of faith we can ensure that the blessedness of others is recognised. We can offer some of the 'reward' that will be fulfilled in the kingdom of God: when our neighbour is mourning, we can offer some measure of comfort; when our neighbour hungers and thirsts for righteousness, we can work with them for justice.

We can show mercy to those who are merciful. Such actions are the signs of the kingdom of God already among us. The Beatitudes further elucidate what it means to love and to be a neighbour.

There is a story of a man who decided that he would convert to Judaism as soon as he could find a Rabbi who could recite the whole Torah while standing on one foot. The man approached one Rabbi and asked if the Rabbi would recite the Torah while standing on one foot. The Rabbi laughed and told the man his request was absurd. The man met another Rabbi and made the same request. That Rabbi just shook his head and walked away. The man then heard of another Rabbi and went to him and asked him to recite the Torah while standing on one foot. Immediately, the Rabbi stood on one foot. Then he proclaimed, 'You shall love the Lord your God with all your heart, with all your soul and all your mind, and you shall love your neighbour as yourself.' Then the Rabbi stopped and stood on both of his feet. He was finished.

The man said to the Rabbi, 'Surely that is not the whole of the Torah!' To which the Rabbi replied, 'Ah, it is the heart of the Torah. All of the rest is commentary.'

All of the Commandments and all of the requirements that flow from each of them are commentary on the ways we love God and neighbour. It is important commentary, to be sure, with all of the misunderstandings of love that abound. The Commandments, the Beatitudes and all of Jesus' teachings help us to understand what love really is and how to live in love. How do we define love? To whom do we point as an example of one who loves God and neighbour? As we form our children, youth and adults in Christian morality, how do we continually connect the 'commentary' with the heart of Christian morality?

In John's Gospel we read that at the Last Supper Jesus taught about love as he washed the feet of his disciples. 'So if I, your Lord and Teacher, have washed your feet, you also ought to wash one another's feet. For I have set you an example, that you also should do as I have done to you' (John 13:14-15).

When I taught young people at a Catholic school, we would prepare for the Holy Thursday liturgy a few days before that celebration. I explained that the foot washing at the liturgy was symbolic, but it was a 'sterilised' version of the reality of the Last Supper – I know in our parish people carefully washed and groomed their feet before the Holy Thursday service! Then I talked about the probable reality of the disciples' feet at the Last Supper. The Holy Land is a hot and dusty place and the disciples wore sandals. Their feet must have been really dirty! Foot washing was not only the task of a servant, it was the job of the lowest of the servants in the house.

I would ask the students what they thought were the worst chores that they saw people doing around the school and the parish. They named what they saw: cleaning the boys' bathroom, washing out the garbage bins, dusting the tops of lockers. And then we did those chores in memory of Jesus, trying on our role as servants to others. When the chores were finished, I washed the students' hands and spoke to each of them as I did. I spoke of what their hands might do for the Lord. Strong hands, gentle hands, artistic hands can all express love of God and neighbour.

After he washed the disciples' feet, Jesus gave them a new commandment. 'I give you a new commandment, that you love one another. Just as I have loved you, you also should love one another' (John 13:34).

We are to grow beyond loving our neighbour as we love ourselves; we are to love others as Jesus has loved us. We may know how to wash feet and be happy to serve others, but Jesus did more than that. He gave himself to his followers. Would they understand the way he loved more fully after the events of Good Friday?

Later during the Last Supper, Jesus gave them an idea of the kind of love he had for them, and the kind of love he was asking of them. Jesus said, 'No one has greater love than this, to lay down one's life for one's friend' (John 15:13).

Sometimes, I think that, for us, 'laying down' our lives has more to do with how we live our lives than with dying for those we love. The daily living of love, the serving, the forgiving, are all ways that we 'lay down our lives'. We may suffer too, and we all know stories of people who have given their lives – have died – for their family or their country or a cause of justice. How do you lay down your life in love?

Forming our children in Christian morality means that we teach them the social doctrines of the Church. These doctrines, rooted in the life and teachings of Jesus, are the Church's application of his teachings to contemporary issues. We are to live in love by promoting the dignity of the human person in all situations;

by working for justice and the rights of workers; by speaking for those who cannot protect themselves. These efforts towards peace and justice and equality are no more popular than they were in Jesus' time. We may, indeed, face opposition and rejection as he did.

Some of my students decided to work for social justice by distributing respect for life literature at the local railway station. I encouraged them and when they completed their mission, they returned to me. They complained, 'Why didn't you tell us what it would be like? People yelled nasty things at us and some ripped up the pamphlets and some spat at us.' I simply replied, 'That is what it may be like sometimes as you live your faith beyond the safe confines of your parish and school.' We have to support one another, pray together and reflect again on Jesus' life in order to have the strength and courage we need.

Moral formation enables us, and those we teach, to make choices that show love for God and others. It helps us, too, to reflect on the choices we have made, and see when we have been loving and when we have failed in love. No moral formation is complete without the assurance of God's mercy and the grace of reconciliation.

Throughout their years together, Jesus had showed his disciples what love meant. He had taught them to love God and neighbour. The new dimension of this teaching is that they were to love each other as he had loved them. And he says, 'By this everyone will know that you are my disciples, if you have love for another.' Sometimes we put all sorts of 'faith' requirements on young people – or even on each other and our fellow parishioners – but do we hold love as the hallmark of the disciple of Jesus Christ? Do we measure our own discipleship in love?

It is good to recall Paul's first letter to the Corinthians. Paul knew that love was the goal, not the talents we have or the powers we have or the knowledge we have gained. Paul learned well what Jesus had taught. If I 'do not have love, I am nothing' (1 Corinthians 13:2).

For Reflection

How do the Commandments and the Beatitudes help you to live with love for God and neighbour?

If someone asked you what is most important in Christian morality, how would you answer?

Would we be happy if our children loved each other as we have loved them? How would they act?

Chapter VII

'I have set you an example'
(John 13:15)

Jesus called his disciples, and he calls us, as individuals. But his call does not end there; he calls us as individuals into a community of his disciples. As the *General Directory for Catechesis* says, 'Christian community life is not recognised spontaneously' (GDC 86). This may seem like an understatement to anyone who has lived in a community! Shared life does not happen spontaneously, in fact it does not happen slowly or at all unless we are committed to living together and to working at all that Christian community life requires.

The first Christian community life we share in is with our family, in the domestic church of our homes. Certainly, Christian family life does not spontaneously occur! There is the relationship between a man and a woman that grows into love and seeks commitment. There is the Sacrament of Matrimony the couple confers on each other, perhaps still in the 'love is blind' stage. Then, blinkers off, the couple begins the daily challenges of living in love. There are joys, but there are sacrifices too, the little – and sometimes big – adjustments they must make in order to share life and space.

If God blesses the couple with children, there are further adjustments. The Christian community life of new parents is unbelievably happy, yet incredibly challenging. This new member requires constant care and attention, sometimes all night long. Schedules change and priorities change and sometimes the financial responsibilities mean the couple has to cut back on things they have enjoyed or would like to have.

Growing in Christian community life within the family happens gradually for the children who are born or adopted into it. In small steps, as they grow more independent, children are asked to share in the chores and to also make sacrifices for their brothers and sisters and the good of the family.

Extended family is part of a family's Christian community life as well. For some families this means actually sharing their home and daily life with grandparents or other relatives. Other families visit extended family to share joys and sorrows; many families offer care for relatives who are ill, especially if they are elderly or live alone. In reaching out to extended family, there is compromise, both for wife and husband, who each have relatives.

Even looking only at the Christian community life of families, we see there are challenges. When it comes to the Church community, then, it is easy to see why the *General Directory for Catechesis* says catechesis is to form us 'to live in community and to participate actively in the life and mission of the Church' (GDC 86).

We live not only in the family community, but also in the larger community of faith – for most of us this is our parish. Of course we do not 'live' with this larger community in the same way we live in family. We share life in a different way and this sharing life also requires love and patience, compromise and sacrifice.

The German theologian Dietrich Bonhoeffer wrote about life in Christian community. He said it is good to have a dream of what the community can be, to hold an ideal. However, he wisely pointed out that if we love our dream of community more than the reality of our community, we can destroy it.

Jesus must have had a dream for what his community of disciples would be. Wouldn't he have hoped for loving relationships, faithfulness and mutual understanding and loyalty? If Jesus had loved the dream of community more than the reality, the Scriptures would be very different. The original twelve disciples would have been replaced when they failed to live up to Jesus' dream. Perhaps any disciples who failed to understand Jesus' teachings, who criticised Jesus' dining with sinners or whose mother sought a place of honour for them would have been excluded. It can give us great comfort to know that even Jesus' closest friends did not always live community well.

The reality of the Christian community is that we are all sinners. And the foundation of our living together is not that we like each other or that we always agree with each other. The foundation of Christian community is Jesus Christ who called us together. That is a critical belief that we hold and share with our children.

The very idea of community is particularly counter-cultural in an age of extreme individualism. There are 'reality' television programmes in which people compete and choose who can stay in the game. The contestants can vote each other off of an island or out of a house. There is also a game show host who eliminates contestants by declaring, 'You are the weakest link'.

Formation for Christian community life embraces a number of aspects. We learn to honour each member's God-given dignity, but to honour one another's dignity we must appreciate our own dignity. As parents and teachers, it is important to foster self-esteem in our children. We can do this by helping them to identify their gifts and by providing ways for them to use those gifts in service to others.

There are people who have great gifts of music, dance or art, and these may be easy to recognise and affirm. However, there are other gifts – the ability to listen, make people laugh or feel welcome – that need to be named, affirmed and called into service.

But we also form children – and grow ourselves – in community life as we, and they, learn to name the gifts which others bring. Competition can be healthy in sports and games, but such competition can also teach us that there are winners and losers. This can be translated into a feeling that my talents are only good if they can beat yours.

What gifts do you see in other members of your parish? We might make this a topic for a family conversation to foster awareness of the many gifts that people bring to the Church community. We can encourage our children to focus on the gifts and abilities that their peers have to move them beyond any competitive stance towards others.

It saddened me when I would ask my students to make a list of their gifts and they would stare at the blank paper, unable to identify any gifts they found in themselves. That is when I learned that we all need others to recognise our gifts and call them forth. I did this recognising and calling forth for my students very intentionally. They became more confident in naming their gifts and being eager to use them in our projects to serve others.

A next step with those students was to help them see and name each other's gifts. At first, they named some rather 'generic' gifts: 'Megan is nice'. While being nice is laudable, I wanted them to see more in each other and to see the many gifts with which God endows his people. They learned and were able to name gifts more precisely. As we would work together in a service effort, I would hear them say, 'We need someone strong to carry the boxes of food – Richard would be perfect!' or, 'Katie, you can sew! Would you make the costumes?'

We are not in competition in community life. Having children work cooperatively – with a partner or in groups – helps us to see how our gifts can help each other. The community, and the mission it serves, needs all of our gifts. Community life thrives when we are able to appreciate each other's gifts.

The Christian community is to be welcoming of all people, even as Jesus was. We all, it seems, have notions of who 'we' are. Think for a moment: who is included when you say 'we'? Our 'we' includes family, most likely, and extended family. It may also include close friends and some of our neighbours.

'We' may include people of our socio-economic group or those who share the same cultural or racial heritage. When we speak of 'we', we may be including members of our parish or some community organisation to which we belong.

Saying 'we' sometimes implies that there is a 'they', who are not included. 'Us' does not include 'them'. Sometimes our attitude towards 'them' is apathy; sometimes it is hostility. If Christian community life is to thrive and grow, it is important to examine who is included in our 'we' and who is not. In expanding the sense of 'we', the community becomes more welcoming and better able to spread the Good News.

Jesus was often criticised for being inclusive. His own followers had a sense of 'we' and it didn't include public sinners. Jesus dined with tax collectors, engaged in conversation with women, touched lepers, welcomed children and proclaimed his message to Samaritans and non-Jews. The disciples' sense of 'we' was exploded – expanded beyond recognition. Jesus came for all people, and some folks desired greater exclusivity.

I grew up in an all-white suburb. 'We' were mostly people of Irish and German descent. 'We' were Catholic and middle class. Then I taught school in an all African-American community. 'We' now included my African-American colleagues, students and their families. It included people who were very poor and many who were not Catholic. Then I worked at a parish in one of the richest suburban areas. 'We' were of many nationalities and wealthy. And so in each experience and in every turn of my life, the Lord has called me to conversion, to another expansion of 'we'.

Children I have taught have no difficulty naming 'us' and 'them'. As I invited them to expand their hearts and to be more inclusive, they readily named who they excluded and considered 'them'. Some of the students named new teachers in the school as 'them'; others named the students who did not attend the parish school but were in religious education sessions instead.

My students and I then considered ways we might welcome these people into our sense of 'we', into this Christian community's life. They were most creative in their responses! The students who named the new kindergarteners as 'them' decided they would each 'adopt' a kindergartener. They devised a whole ceremony, and then planned monthly gatherings, which included a tour of the school and introductions, a tour of the church and planned playground activities that they did together. Those who named the religious education students wrote welcome notes to them for the first session of their classes and left a treat that they had made. Later in the year, the religious education students reciprocated and left notes and treats for the school kids. The sense of who 'we' are grew for everyone.

How do our children experience our welcoming 'them' into our homes? That is their first lesson in the hospitality that is required of Jesus' disciples. We cannot spread the Good News through closed doors – or closed hearts.

Sometimes it is fellow Catholics to whom we need to be more welcoming. We may need to consider welcoming those who do not agree with all of our opinions, or who have irritated us in the past, or those who are new to the community. If we are to teach our children, youth and adults to be welcoming, we must begin with setting a good example.

As members of the Christian community we are called to welcome not just other Catholics, but other Christians as well. How do we reach out in ecumenical efforts that respond to Jesus' prayer 'that all may be one'? How do we teach our children that our embrace of other Christians is part of our Catholic identity? And, as Catholics, we are to respect people of other faiths. That respect comes as we learn – and as we teach our children – about other people's beliefs and as we remember that we are all children of one God.

Expanding our sense of 'we' and welcoming all people is the way we witness to the Lord and begin to share the Good News more broadly. And that sharing of the Good News of Jesus Christ is the mission of the Christian community. Is the welcome mat out in our parish? Is it out for those who are 'different' from us in whatever ways that may be? Is the welcome mat out for those who have disabilities? Often people cannot go to church because there is no access for one who cannot walk easily or who uses a wheelchair for mobility.

Do we provide for those who are challenged with developmental disabilities or who cannot hear? What about a welcome mat in another language for people who come to us from different countries?

In the formation of Christian community life, we can point out to our children the ways our parish provides for the needs of the community members so that they feel welcomed and can participate fully. As families we can raise issues of accessibility when we see they are inadequate. And we can be the ones who offer a lift to church to someone who lives alone and does not drive. We can be the ones who help an elderly person up the church steps. In these simple ways, we welcome others in Jesus' name and our children see and learn.

In today's world, I think we need more than a welcome mat at the door, since many people, even our fellow Catholics, do not come to the church. The Christian community, if it is to be strong and to grow, needs to have what I would call an 'aggressive welcome mat'. That is, we need to carry our welcome to where people are. Some Catholics have been hurt by the Church, some have merely drifted away and some have felt unwelcome and been welcomed elsewhere. How do we go to those people to offer healing, reconnection, or the simple 'we miss you' that can make a difference?

The more the Christian community focuses on spreading the Good News through their efforts at welcoming and being inclusive, the less time there is for the bickering that starts when we have lost a sense of mission. If the Church – the parish – is focused only on internal issues, we lose the vision of why Jesus called us together in the first place.

Once there was a pastor who was interviewing a priest to be his associate, so he brought the priest to see the church. I was in the church and my students were scattered throughout the church praying and journaling.

At one point I heard the pastor say, 'This is the church. Of course, it is much nicer without the people'. I am sure he didn't mean what his words seemed to imply, but I suppose we have all, in our weak moments, had the thought that the church is great, if only there weren't people in it!

Our likes and dislikes, our 'we' and 'they', can inhibit the kingdom of God. And so we need grace to live life in the Christian community and to welcome one another in love. We are not, after all, inviting people to just be our friends, we are inviting people to meet Jesus Christ in this community of faith. God graces us for this work.

It is important to remember that our efforts are intended to search out and welcome back those who have left us, not to increase the Sunday collection. We seek to bring people back to the Christian community because the Church is the Body of Christ. When members of the community are missing we are incomplete. Paul wrote to the Corinthians about the Christian community, 'As it is, there are many members yet one body. The eye cannot say to the hand, "I have no need of you" nor again the head to the feet, "I have no need of you" (1 Corinthians 12:20-21). Therefore, we in the Christian community need one another.

Paul also wrote, 'There are varieties of gifts, but the same Spirit; and there are varieties of services, but the same Lord; and there are varieties of activities, but it is the same God who activates all of them in everyone. To each is given the manifestation of the Spirit for the common good' (1 Corinthians 12:4-7). We each belong to the Body of Christ, but we have different roles in the Christian community. Part of our formation for life in the Christian community is an understanding of and appreciation for our own role and the roles of others.

In our parishes there are different ministries in which people serve. The parishes have ordained ministers and lay people who serve in ministries of catechesis, or in liturgical ministries, or in the many works that the parish does for the poor and those in need. We can model appreciation and gratitude for all that these people do 'for the common good' and encourage our children to do the same.

We do have certain roles and we do live in a faith community that has a hierarchy. Sometimes I think this impacts on our notion of who should thank whom. I know people who expect a thank you when they volunteer at the parish, but never offer a thank you to their priest. Some people critique something that is going on in the parish, but instead of working to correct it, they expect the priest to do it. We are all one body and each member needs encouragement. When was the last time you thanked your priest or offered to pray for him? We can pray as a family for all those who serve in our parish and all the members of the Christian community in which we share.

There are roles in the Christian community beyond the parish of course. The bishops and the pope need our prayers and encouragement as well. The missionaries who serve in distant lands and all the members of the whole Church need our prayers.

It is important to remember, and to teach our children, that the Christian community is much bigger than our little community. We can forget that the reality of the Church is in places all around the world and that some of our fellow Catholics cannot practise their faith openly, and that some struggle with terrible conditions of poverty and oppression. Remembering them can help us overcome our disappointment that our parish fundraiser was a failure.

Embracing one another and welcoming all people to our life in Christian community certainly does not mean there are no disagreements among us.

In fact, we are not only to comfort each other but to challenge each other with the gospel message as well. Even Peter and Paul disagreed. But we come together, as Peter and Paul did, and with the Holy Spirit's guidance come to a decision that is best for the People of God.

Teaching our children to articulate their concerns and to measure decisions against the values Jesus proclaimed prepares them to be active members of the community of faith. Teaching them to settle disagreements with kindness and for the good of the family helps them to disagree fairly and to keep the good of all as the goal.

The *General Directory for Catechesis* (see GDC 86) spells out the attitudes that we are to develop and foster through catechesis. The attitudes it names are based on Jesus' teachings as recorded in the Gospel of Matthew. The first attitudes we are to have in order to live in Christian community are simplicity and humility. It is easy to see the importance of these attitudes. We cannot live well in community if we are steeped in self-importance and feel superior to others.

The second attitude is concern for the 'least' among us, whether these 'least' be children, or the poor, or the elderly. Who is 'least' in our parish? Is it the single parent? Is it the divorced woman? Is it the school dropout? Is it the person who suffers from alcoholism or another addiction? How can we teach concern for these people and not judgement? Who do our children see as 'least' and how do we assist them to reach out in concern? Perhaps we have heard them make fun of the child who is slower in school or someone on their team who does not play well. We might suggest that they offer to help the classmate who struggles academically or that they practise their sport with the child less gifted in athletics.

Can we remind our children – and ourselves – that Jesus identified himself with those who are considered 'least' among the community?

A third attitude for community life is that we offer particular care for those who are alienated. People can become alienated from the Christian community for various reasons. Some of the reasons may seem trite: 'They criticised the flowers I planted in the parish yard'.

Some people's reasons for alienation can be traced back to a bad experience in confession or to the poor treatment of their child by other children or even by a teacher. Other people have experienced alienation because of profound events that have shaken their faith and destroyed their trust in the Church. Sometimes we are aware of a person's reason for alienation, other times we are not. Whatever the reason, we can seek to ease the pain and offer compassion. In cases of alienation, as in all our neighbours' experiences, we are reminded by Jesus, 'Do not judge ... the measure you give will be the measure you get' (Matthew 7:1-2).

Another attitude to consider in the Christian community is called fraternal correction. As parents, we do not have a problem correcting our child when he or she is doing wrong. That, we know, is how they learn. It is much more difficult, however, to think about correcting other adults. The attitude of fraternal correction flows from our call to live as Jesus taught us to live. When we fail in this, we often recognise our own failure and make the necessary adjustments to our behaviour. Fraternal correction is risky business, for we do not judge, yet we offer, in love, correction. We can set a good example and sometimes this is enough. In other cases, we may speak with the person to remind him or her of their dignity and our concern.

Listening is always a part of such efforts, since we may misunderstand something we saw or heard. We may not be aware of the factors in a person's life that have led to acts contrary to the gospel.

The ways in which we offer correction to our children sets a good example for how they deal with others. Do we listen to their story? Do we do correcting always in the context of love rather than when we are angry? Is our concern for them paramount and not the opinion of the neighbours who saw their misdeed? Do we respect their dignity even as we endeavour to help them change their actions? We can pray with them and for them, as we should for anyone who is struggling to live the gospel.

The next attitude the *General Directory* names is, in fact, common prayer. In Matthew's Gospel we read, 'Again, truly I tell you, if two of you agree on earth about anything you ask, it will be done for you by my Father in heaven. For where two or three are gathered in my name, I am there among them' (Matthew 18:19-20). If we have a prayerful attitude towards one another and engage in prayer with one another, we build up the Christian community and enrich its life.

The next attitude cited is one that we understand is necessary in any relationship: mutual forgiveness. Even in relationships that we have chosen and entered into with love, we will always have times when we hurt, disappoint or cause pain for the other person. We seek forgiveness; we offer forgiveness. We do this because the relationship and our love for each other is deeper than the hurt.

In the Christian community, we are together with people we have not chosen to be with. We have not called these people, the Lord has called them. And we have been called by the Lord, not by the other members of the community.

We may take offense and give offense more easily, even unintentionally, because we do not know each other well or know each person's vulnerabilities. Recognising our need for forgiveness can help us to develop a generosity of forgiveness towards others.

How do we offer forgiveness to our children? Do they see that we can forgive and move past hurts? We can help our children to be forgivers who know that holding a grudge only hurts themselves. We can teach them that disciples of Jesus do not seek retaliation for wrongs done to them.

There are times when we offend each other and we do not even know we have done so. Part of the problem, it seems, is that we sometimes impute motives to each other's actions that were not the motives at all. We have all heard of giving someone 'the benefit of the doubt'. When we don't know why someone has done something that has hurt us, we are open to learning the reason they did what they did before concluding that it was intentional. I heard a preacher invite people to go a step beyond that posture. He said we should offer one another 'benevolent interpretation'. That is, assume the best intention for someone's behaviour rather than the worst. Suppose you are driving on a major roadway and another driver comes speeding up and cuts you off. You can offer benevolent interpretation, which goes something like this: 'Oh dear, someone they know must be really ill to be in such a hurry!' No easy task, this offering benevolent interpretation. But wouldn't it be nice to think that other people were interpreting our actions in this benevolent fashion? How would it change our family or our parish or our community if we always assumed the best of each other? And if we discover that a benevolent interpretation is, in fact, wrong and we are hurt or have hurt another, may we let forgiveness flow. We can teach our children to look at people and see their goodness. We can teach them that, for all the faults and failings each of us has, we are still images of God.

The final attitude the *Directory* names is really where we must begin if we are to live in Christian community: love. The love we have for one another in the Christian community is not a 'feeling', though at times it may be; it is not always 'liking', though at times it can be. The love we live in the Christian community is a reflection of God's love for us. The love we live in Christian community is a commitment and not merely a sentiment. It is a love that attends to God's Word; a love that is nourished with the Eucharist; a love that celebrates our faith together; a love that, in small ways and large ways, bids us to lay down our lives.

As we grow – and form our children, youth and adults – as members of the Christian community, we grow in the holiness to which all the baptised are called. We develop not just attitudes, but virtues that are both the source and the fruit of life together. We can help each other to grow in faith, hope and love. And that is no small thing.

Of course, the cross is present in Christian community and we may even be 'slivers' to each other at times as we journey with and to the Lord. He told us that if we are to be his disciples, we should expect crosses, but we can help one another to bear whatever crosses each one must carry.

The cost of Christian community life is the same cost that is expected of family life: to live not just with each other, but *for* each other; to forgive and to try again each day to love more fully and give more generously to each other. These are a small price to pay to live in the kingdom of God.

For Reflection

What in Christian community life gives you the most joy? How do you share that joy with your children?

What in Christian community life do you find the most challenging? How do you teach your children to meet the challenges of living in community?

The *General Directory of Catechesis* presents attitudes for living in Christian community. What other attitude is critical for your own parish community today?

Chapter VIII

'Go, therefore, and make disciples'
(Matthew 28:19)

Jesus did not choose twelve disciples who were already fully prepared to go and make disciples. They must have been good men, after all, they responded to Jesus' call immediately. They left their jobs and loved ones and went with this man whom they had just met.

But the Scriptures tell us of their failures to understand Jesus' message sometimes. Peter was overeager on occasion. They argued about which of them was to be considered the greatest. The mother of the sons of Zededee, James and John, asked if her sons could have the best seats in Jesus' kingdom. I have always wondered if the sons put their mother up to asking this of Jesus.

We know from Scripture that, for all their goodness and dedication to Jesus, they fell asleep when he asked them to pray with him; we know they deserted him and that Peter denied knowing Jesus at all. But Jesus knew them and he loved them. He trusted that these disciples would carry on his work eventually. And he knew how to prepare them to do that work.

From the time Jesus called his first disciples together, he was forming them to share in his mission. Jesus lived among them and they journeyed with him along the roads as he ministered. His disciples were with him as he taught the crowds and Jesus often explained his teachings and parables to them in private. When they misunderstood what he did or said, he corrected them. Over and over, he told them not to be afraid.

Jesus prayed when he was with his disciples, taught them to pray and prayed for them. Jesus gave the twelve disciples, 'power and authority over all demons and to cure diseases' and sent them 'to proclaim the kingdom of God and to heal' (Luke 9:1-2). He sent seventy other disciples to go ahead of him to the places where he would be going and told them to travel in pairs.

Jesus gave the disciples a final lesson at the Last Supper as he washed their feet and told them that as the leaders, they were to be servants. He gave himself to them in the breaking of the bread. He suffered and died for them and for all people, and rose victorious. His followers witnessed the proof of all that Jesus was and all that he taught.

He returned to his disciples after the resurrection and ate with them and offered them his peace. Then Jesus is going to ascend to his Father. And after all of the ways he had prepared his disciples, he gives them a mission:

> Go, therefore, and make disciples of all nations, baptising them in the name of the Father and of the Son and of the Holy Spirit, and teaching them to obey everything that I have commanded you. And remember, I am with you always, to the end of the age. (Matthew 28:19-20)

Before he ascended to the Father, Jesus told the disciples again that the Holy Spirit would come to them: 'I am sending upon you what my Father promised; so stay here in the city until you have been clothed with power from on high' (Luke 24:49).

After Jesus' death, the disciples were afraid. They must have felt lost and alone. Even after Mary Magdalene's encounter with the risen Christ and the other post-resurrection appearances of Jesus, the disciples were not running through the streets proclaiming Jesus. But they had also been told to stay in Jerusalem until the Holy Spirit came to them.

In the *Acts of the Apostles* we read of the Pentecost event when the promised Spirit came to the disciples and they were strengthened and took to the streets. They preached and healed and invited people to know Jesus and follow him. They performed signs and wonders, and they were persecuted. The disciples were doing the mission that Jesus gave them and the community of believers grew.

Jesus, the *General Directory* says, 'proclaimed the Kingdom of God as the urgent and definitive intervention of God in history'. This is the Good News that Jesus proclaimed. And the *Directory* goes on to say, 'To this Gospel, Jesus devoted his entire earthly life: he made known the joy of belonging to the Kingdom, its demands, its *magna carta*, the mysteries which it embraces, the life of fraternal charity of those who enter it and its future fulfilment' (GDC 34).

The mission of Jesus, first entrusted to the apostles, is now the mission of the Church. As the Church's document on evangelisation tells us, the Church 'exists in order to evangelise' (EN 14). It is not that the Church has a mission; the mission has a Church – a community of believers – who carry on the mission of Jesus Christ.

Through the Sacraments of Christian Initiation we were given responsibility for this mission. We are children of God who share in the life of the Blessed Trinity and are sealed with the Holy Spirit and nourished with the Eucharist. These gifts have been given to us not for our own satisfaction, but that we might serve. We are called to witness to our faith and to 'participate in the apostolic and missionary activity of the People of God' (CCC 1270).

In Baptism we received a candle and were told, 'You have been enlightened by Christ. Walk always as children of the light and keep the flame of faith alive in your hearts' (*Rite of Baptism*). These words echo Jesus' words to his followers, 'You are the light of the world' (Matthew 5:14). As the late Pope John Paul said, when speaking of the light of Christ, 'Ours is the wonderful and demanding task of becoming its reflection'.

We are to be light for the world today. What kind of light does the world need? We have lights, of course: neon lights and the lights of computer screens and video games. What kind of light is 'the light of the world'?

I asked the children in my religious education group to think about what kind of light they could be for the world as Jesus' disciples. One boy said he would be a refrigerator light, because if people 'opened him up' he would shine. Another said she would be candlelight because it is soft and would not show people's defects so much. Another wanted to be like a stoplight so he could help people see when to go ahead with what they were doing and when to stop. Some wanted to be flashing warning lights to keep people from danger and doing bad things. And one girl wanted to be the light of a campfire because people could gather around her and tell their stories and she would listen and try to make them feel good about themselves.

What kind of light are you? How do you reflect the light of Christ for others? Our children see the light we bring and learn to be light too, to not only share the Good News, but to be the good news for others. With the Church community, they, and we, carry on the mission of Jesus.

Adults who receive Baptism are given initial formation for the mission of the Church and may begin to serve that mission soon after their initiation. They continue, however, to grow in understanding of that mission and in their ability to spread the Good News. Those who are baptised as infants or very young children do not leave the baptismal font and begin evangelising.

As Jesus' first followers needed the formation he gave them before he sent them on their mission, we, too, need preparation for this mission. And that preparation is ongoing as we continue to grow in faith and to experience conversion at various times throughout our lives. We continue our formation for mission in many ways: in family life, through experiences of joy and loss, and in situations at work and in our communities.

Catechesis forms us for mission. The sixth task of catechesis cited in the *General Directory* is 'missionary initiation'. In fact, the other five tasks – knowledge, prayer, liturgical formation, moral formation and formation for life in Christian community – are all forming us for the mission of Jesus Christ. We need all of these dimensions of our faith if we are to witness to and proclaim the Good News in our world today.

As we teach our children, youth and adults to carry on the mission of Jesus Christ with the Church, we have to offer a holistic formation.

In virtue of its own internal dynamic, the faith demands to be known, celebrated, lived and translated into prayer. Catechesis must cultivate each of these dimensions. The faith, however, is lived out by the Christian community and proclaimed in mission; it is a shared and proclaimed faith. These dimensions must also be encouraged by catechesis. (GDC 84)

What kind of preparation does one need to take on a new task? A friend of mine was an experienced glider pilot and invited me to go flying with him. For one who had only flown on large commercial jets, it was a very different experience. First of all, I was certainly not accustomed to arriving at the hanger and helping to push the plane out! I had never experienced a plane that had only two seats or that had to be towed by a truck in order to take off. I did not know that glider planes rode air currents, and even if I had known, it would not have prepared me for the dizzying flight we took. As we spun around and around in circles on the air currents, I began to feel ill and terribly weak. In the midst of this, my friend, the pilot, shouted back to me, 'I'm turning the controls over to you!' If he had turned around and beheld my greenish countenance, he might have thought better of it before he made the move. I was now ill and petrified and he had no idea.

We sometimes 'hand over the controls' to someone and give them something to do for the mission of Jesus – but sometimes we have not looked at the person or listened to what they're saying. We fail to realise that the one receiving this responsibility is not ready. The person may need more encouragement; he or she may need further skills in order to have the confidence to 'take the controls'.

As parents, we seem to know instinctively the preparation our children need before they can do something on their own. We leave the training wheels on the bike until the child has developed the skill of balancing. We show them how to make the bed or to plant a flower. We do it with them so then they can do it on their own.

We may help an elderly neighbour with garden work and take our child along when we go. When a child is old enough, we may show him or her how to help. Our adolescent children may take on the task of helping the neighbour without us.

This is a natural progression of teaching: we demonstrate the lesson or task for the learners, we mentor them in doing the task and then they do the task on their own. Although, as parents and teachers, we have certainly also experienced that our children teach us as well – in life and in faith. We can often be amazed at children's insights and realise what Jesus meant when he said we should become like them.

Our son, Nicholas, was about three years old when he stood in front of his dad and, with a hand gesture that went far above his head, measured himself against his height. 'I am almost as tall as you are, Daddy', he declared. My husband replied, 'Not quite, Nicky, but you are growing'. Nick looked up at his Dad, then down at the floor and thought for a moment.

Finally, undaunted, Nick said, 'But, Daddy, my feet go all the way down to yours'. Nick had reminded me, even at his tender age, that we are all indeed equal in God's sight and stand on the same ground before him.

We do seem to teach life skills and academic content in ways that are attentive to children's needs. We need to be as attentive to their age and development and maturity as we form them in faith. We cannot effectively form them for the mission of Jesus

Christ if we do not know them, or know their concerns and joys, their fears and hopes. We need to listen to those who are being formed in faith.

Parents and teachers can pray together with children, taking the lead and inviting them into the prayer. As the children learn to pray, they may say the prayer with us. When they have learned to pray, we can invite them to lead the family or the class in prayer.

Catechesis prepares us, and our children, to engage in the mission of Jesus. As we teach our children, we cannot 'take the training wheels off' too soon, because they will fall and perhaps never get on a bicycle again.

On the other hand, we can err in the other direction also. We can keep the training wheels on long after they are necessary and not allow them to practise what they have learned. They may beg to have the little wheels removed.

If we decline to remove the wheels when the children are ready to do what they learned, they may lose their desire for cycling and decide they would rather walk.

The organisation Habitat for Humanity, which renovates and builds houses for poor families, was working in my city a few years ago. I decided to volunteer. When I arrived at the burned-out house that we were going to reconstruct, I signed in and awaited instruction. I figured there would be an in-service on the plan, the tools and the process we would use. But, as soon as I signed in, the leader said, 'You can work with Sadie over there and remove that doorframe and build a new one'. Sadie was eighty-two years old. She was high up on a ladder and was wielding a crowbar as if she were twenty. I was thrown into the work, but not alone – Sadie apprenticed me and mentored me as I worked with her. She didn't say, 'You just watch'; nor did she say, 'Do it yourself'. It is a delicate balance giving our children, youth and adults enough formation that they are able to engage in sharing the Good News, yet not requiring so much preparation before they can participate that they lose interest.

What do we and our children need in order to be evangelisers, to be proclaimers of the Good News in witness of life and through words? We do have to know who Jesus Christ is, certainly, and to love him. If we are to share the Good News we have to be able to articulate in whom and in what we believe.

But besides teaching our children the knowledge, the need and the words to express their beliefs, we can offer times to practise sharing their faith. Children can share their faith at home and with their peers in catechetical sessions.

They might be asked to teach something they have learned to younger children, like a prayer perhaps or what we, as Catholics, do during Advent. They can practise engaging in Jesus' mission through apprenticeships with older members of the family or from the parish. They might work side by side with the adult community in a parish food drive. Older children may apprentice to a parish liturgical minister and learn the skills of being a lector or extraordinary minister of Holy Communion. However, I do not think children should replace adults in these roles, except perhaps at a Mass that is celebrated for a group of children who are preparing for Confirmation or some other special occasion. When children take on these roles regularly at the Sunday liturgy, adults tend to relinquish them altogether.

We, and our children, are called to do the mission of Jesus beyond the parish community. The *General Directory* reminds us that formation for mission 'seeks to equip the disciples of Jesus to be present as Christians in society through their professional, cultural and social lives' (GDC 86).

Parents and teachers witness to the ways this 'being present as Christians' happens when they act with justice in their workplaces; when they do not engage in social groups that are prejudiced or racist. Our children see the ways we are present in society: they know who we spend time with, as we know who their friends are, and they are very aware of whether our behaviour with our friends and colleagues is witnessing to Jesus and to our faith.

When I wanted my students to share the Good News beyond the parish, I provided opportunities. They visited the businesses in our village and brought a gift they had made and thanked the owners and workers for the service they provided to the people of the village. Another 'mission' was to visit the people who resided in the local nursing home, and the younger children who could not go visiting made special placemats for the home's dining room. Sometimes I asked my students to do something special for the members of one of our sports teams; other times I asked them to bring a treat for the opposing team.

In all of these and many other ways, these young people engaged in the Works of Mercy and social justice and contributed to the mission of Jesus Christ and the Church. Each time they returned from spreading the Good News, we would gather to pray, reflect and share the experience and to recall what Jesus did and asks us to do. We encouraged one another in our discipleship and in the mission.

We are formed for mission through all of the dimensions of catechesis. And each of the tasks requires both learning and doing. In faith formation, we do not just learn about things, we *do* them: we pray, we celebrate, we make good choices and we live in community. And so, formation for mission cannot end with talking about what we could do. Sometimes what we do is not well received and we need to remember why we do it and turn to the one who sent us on mission and to the community, which shares the mission for support.

The *General Directory* speaks of the gospel attitudes that Jesus taught his disciples before they went on mission. It says that the formation we offer for mission must nourish these attitudes: '[T]o seek out the lost sheep, proclaim and heal at the same time, to be poor, without money or knapsack; to know how to accept rejection and persecution; to place one's trust in the Father and in the support of the Holy Spirit; to expect no other reward than the joy of working for the Kingdom' (GDC 86).

How do we translate these attitudes into contemporary reality? The image of lost sheep is not difficult to see in today's world. One does not blame or criticise the sheep for getting lost. One does not ask how it got lost; one just goes after it, finds it and brings it back. There are many temptations that can make us lose our way; there are situations that separate people from the flock and which require some healing. Who is lost in life's demands and unable to be with the community, who is lost in grief and is too sad to be with us? How do we seek and find the lost sheep – even in our own families – and be with them until they are ready to rejoin the community?

We are to nourish – in our own hearts and our children's – the desire to proclaim and to heal at the same time. This is an important attitude today when there are those who would proclaim teachings with the intention of hurting others – condemning them, excluding them, stripping them of their dignity in the name of religion. Yes, the gospel we proclaim is a challenge and makes demands of those who want to live it. But that same gospel heals, offers forgiveness, brings new life and gives hope even in the midst of our weaknesses. If proclamation is aimed at people to hurt them and to cause division, it is most assuredly not the Good News that Jesus proclaimed.

How do we adopt and nourish an attitude of being poor: shall we throw out our backpacks and money? I think maybe being poor in spirit requires that I not be overly attached to money or backpacks or any other possessions. But also it requires that we not be dependent on those things for our own happiness or for the mission.

When I was a youth minister in a parish in a very wealthy community, our youth group did a project to provide necessities for poor families in the city. People were asked to bring food items or clothing or to give monetary donations. Parishioners brought an abundance of food items. They brought carloads of brand new clothing and gave large sums of money. None of the adults I approached, however, would go with us to the city to meet some of the families who lived in poverty.

One of the youth members came to the balcony of the church where I was standing, viewing all of the goods that had been stacked in the church. As we gazed on the richness of the treasure below, I said to the young man, 'People were so generous!' And the young man said to me, 'You know, the problem in this community is that people will give stuff but they won't give of themselves'. We live an attitude of being poor when we can give of ourselves and do not let things or money or 'stuff' replace the gift of self in our mission.

Disciples of Jesus must know how to accept rejection. Living the gospel means carrying the cross, and sometimes that cross is rejection – of us and of the Good News we proclaim. That we will experience rejection because of our mission is a given; the question is, how will we face that rejection?

Jesus faced rejection throughout his life: many of the Jewish leaders rejected him; the gospel tells us that he was rejected in Nazareth, his own home town; the rich, young man rejected Jesus' invitation because he had many possessions. There was the man who rejected the immediacy of Jesus' invitation and wanted to go and bury his father before following Jesus.

Jesus could face rejection because he kept his eye on the Father's will and because he prayed. He did not compromise the message he proclaimed to accommodate those who were not ready to respond. Neither did he get angry at those who walked away from him, nor did he ever say to any of them, 'And don't bother coming back'. He always left the door open.

How do our children see us face rejection when we stand up for gospel values? What do we do when we speak up for the needs of others and people get angry at us and say those needy people ought to take care of themselves? How do we respond when we have welcomed a person whom others don't find appealing and so tell us that we are stupid? We can teach our children to keep their eyes on the mission of Jesus and to respond to those who reject them by treating the people who do the rejecting with respect.

In some countries, we would face persecution for being disciples of Jesus Christ. We would not be able to practise our faith openly. And even if a government does not persecute Catholics, we may be persecuted by popular opinion or by those who espouse anti-gospel values. When we face such opposition to spreading the Good News, we can remember our brothers and sisters who are persecuted for the faith and pray for them. We can redouble our support for one another so we do not lose heart.

We and our children are to be formed to trust in the Father and the Holy Spirit. After all, the mission we have is from Jesus, who came to do the Father's will and inaugurate God's kingdom; Jesus' mission was animated by the Holy Spirit. We who continue Jesus' work can rely on being given what we need to do that work just as Jesus was.

The lessons of trust and support are learned first in the home. When we keep our promises to each other and to our children, they learn that they can trust people. When we encourage them and support their efforts, they learn that the help they need will be there for them.

The final attitude the *Directory* names is that we do the mission with no expectation of reward, other than the joy of working for God's kingdom. When the work itself is its own reward, we have reached a maturity of faith.

As my students prepared for the Sacrament of Confirmation, they were asked to 'try on' the life of service to which they were committing themselves. I intentionally did not assign a number of hours they were expected to complete, but I did ask that they think in terms of 'circles of service': to their family, their parish and school, their neighbourhood and the larger community – even on to the city or internationally.

As they began their preparation and were beginning to share what they had done to serve, some of them would immediately ask, 'Does that count?' I knew they were growing in their faith and sense of mission when they no longer asked that question. To help them feel the joy of working for the kingdom, as they recounted what they had done, I asked who was affected by their service. I affirmed what they had done and how they had spread peace or compassion and made a difference, however small, by their work. One student might say, 'I helped my little brother with his homework', so I would draw out the effect that help had on the brother. I would discuss how it helped their parents, who could spend time with each other as a result, and how his help freed his older sister to study for her exam. At the end of their stories of service, we all realised that the world was a bit closer to the kingdom of God because of what they had done. They felt the joy of this and asked for nothing more.

The joy of working for the kingdom has to be evident in our own lives if our children are to seek and be satisfied with that reward. There are challenges in parenthood and in teaching; we may find we are frustrated with the systems in which we live and work, and there may be days when we do not see any results for all of our efforts. In spite of these realities and the 'bad days' we sometimes endure, we know the joy of being a parent or a teacher with the privilege of forming children in the faith.

Unless our children see that there is joy in our faith and in doing the mission of Jesus, will they be attracted to it? I remember reading, a long time ago, that before we go after something in life, we should see how happy the people are who already have what we seek. When our children look at you and me and the rest of the community of faith, do they see the happiness that comes from being children of God and co-workers for the kingdom? As parents and teachers, we can take time to share with our children the joy of something we did to spread the Good News. We can listen to their stories of service to Jesus' mission and celebrate together.

In the Gospel of John, we read the account of Jesus' last discourse to his disciples. He has washed their feet, given them the new commandment and encouraged them to believe in the Father and in him. He promised that the Holy Spirit would come and assured them that the Spirit would remind them of all he had taught them. He told his disciples that they were joined to him and to each other as a vine and its branches. And he said, 'I have said these things to you so that my joy may be in you, and that your joy may be complete.'

Formation for mission of evangelisation – spreading the Good News – includes embracing the joy of doing that mission. Even our efforts to proclaim the Good News will fall short if they are devoid of the joy of that Good News – it may sound like *news*, but it won't sound like *good* news.

Through all of the dimensions of formation in faith, we come to know Jesus Christ and to love him more deeply. The *Catechism* says, 'From this loving knowledge of Christ springs the desire to proclaim him, to "evangelise", and to lead others to the "yes" of faith in Jesus Christ' (CCC 429).

Loving Jesus makes us want to share him and his message with others. And so we eagerly accept the responsibility of our mission as members of his body, the Church.

In recent years, the Church has refocused on its mission of evangelisation. Pope John Paul II spoke of the need for a 'new evangelisation', which included proclaiming the Good News to those who had not heard the Good News of Jesus Christ – the traditional sense of the Church mission 'to all nations'. But the Pope expanded the understanding of evangelisation to include proclaiming the Good News to those who had once heard it, but perhaps the initial proclamation had not been deepened through catechesis. He also included in this need for a new evangelisation those who have heard but forgotten the message of the gospel and those whose faith has grown cold.

When I read the gospels, I feel a sense of urgency in Jesus as he ministers. He is always about the Father's work, even when he was but a child – he was not lost, but teaching in the temple. We see him on the road going to the different villages to teach and to heal; when he does try to get away for a while, people follow him and he teaches again in spite of weariness.

Our world today is in desperate need of Good News. We need only listen to the news or hear our neighbour's troubles to sense the urgent need for the Good News of Jesus to offer hope and comfort and courage. Yet some Catholics have not heard the call to mission or been affirmed in the good works as part of that mission. Perhaps we took it for granted that everyone knew their role in the Church's mission of evangelisation.

I am not sure of the genesis of the sense that I was supposed to help spread the Good News, but I knew it clearly, even as a child. I am sure my family and my teachers, my neighbours and my friends helped to instill that sense. I was meant to share the gift of faith, of that I was certain.

When I was about eight years old, I loved being a Catholic. I was concerned about those who were not Catholic because I heard they would not go to heaven. My parents had friends who were not Catholic and they had a son who was seven years old. I felt very sad that he would not go to heaven, so I decided to do something about it.

I had a small statue of the Infant Jesus of Prague that was made of glow-in-the-dark plastic. When I knew that my parents' friends were coming over with their son, I would put the statue under a lamp early in the morning so it would soak up the light all day. When the company arrived, we would all eat together and then the adults would play a card game and the son and I would be sent off to play – but I had other plans. I would take the boy into our coat closet and shut the door so it was dark. And then, the Infant Jesus of Prague would 'appear' to the boy and talk to him about becoming Catholic.

It was not, in hindsight, a laudable exercise of the mission of Jesus, but I knew that I had something good in my faith and I wanted to share it. I do not want to return to the time before the Church's self-understanding included love and respect for other Church communities, nor do I want to frighten and confuse people in my efforts to proclaim the Good News, as I am sure I did to that little boy. However, there was a passion and a conviction and a joy that I knew, which I hope all will have.

Years after I had moved away, I was invited back to my old home parish to speak to the teachers and catechists. As people were entering the church, I welcomed each one. I spotted two young adults, whom I had taught when they were in primary school, approaching. After I greeted them, I asked, 'What are you doing here tonight?' They replied with enthusiasm, 'We are going to be catechists this year!'

Suddenly I had a flashback to their days in my classroom and found myself wondering, 'What did I teach them? Did I teach them what they need to know to be catechists?' I wanted to sit and talk with them, to ask them questions and try to make up for what I might have failed to teach them. Then I realised that when I taught them, I was clear that I was preparing them to receive the Sacrament of Confirmation; I did not really think that I was helping to form them to be evangelisers. I wanted them to know their faith, but I did not think much about the fact that they would need to share that faith with others.

That is the perspective we should keep in mind as we form our children in faith. We are preparing them to carry on the mission of spreading the Good News. We are preparing evangelisers. No matter how young or old our children are, they will be sharing the Good News, and all of the six dimensions of faith formation that we offer equip them for that mission.

Whatever their age, our children are even now participating in the mission. Think of the ways that, simply in their being, they share joy and excitement and help us to see the beauty and wonder of God's gifts as we look anew through their eyes.

But our children will grow and mature and one day will respond to God's call to a particular vocation through which to live their faith. Part of formation for mission is helping them to explore the vocations of marriage and single life, ordained life and religious life. We can teach them to discern what vocation they are called to and through which they will continue to, 'Go, and make disciples'.

For Reflection

When you reflect on the life of Jesus, what stories of his mission do you find the most powerful for your faith?

Who are the people you see serving the mission of Jesus in your family, your parish and your neighbourhood? How can you affirm them?

Think about a time when you felt the joy of doing the work of spreading the Good News. Share the story of that time with your children.

Chapter IX

'The kingdom of God is among you'
(Luke 17:21)

When you hear the phrase 'kingdom of God', what do you think of? Before Jesus came to earth, people had expectations of what the Messiah would be like and what the Messiah would do. Some people expected that the Messiah would save them from their enemies and establish an earthly kingdom. Even when Jesus came, some of his followers seemed to be influenced by these expectations of earthly victory of some sort. Jesus was a disappointment to some people; he proclaimed the kingdom of God, but it was not what some people had hoped for.

Are we disappointed? And are we comforted or are we challenged as we hear Jesus teach about the kingdom? He said it is hard for those who are wealthy to enter the kingdom and that it belongs to those who are like children. He said the kingdom of God is for the poor in spirit and that those who put a hand to the plow and look back are not fit for the kingdom. And he taught that people from every direction on earth will recline at the table in the kingdom of God.

Jesus used wonderful rich images to describe the kingdom of God. He said the kingdom of God is as if someone scattered seed on the ground and, as day after day passes, the seed sprouts and grows and the one who sowed the seed does not know how it happened. And when it is time, the sower goes out to harvest.

Jesus taught that the kingdom is like a mustard seed that someone sows and it grows into a tree so big that the birds make their home in it. He said the kingdom is like leaven that a woman puts into flour until all of the flour is leavened. Jesus taught that the kingdom of God grows and that it is inclusive.

And, as we read in John's Gospel, Jesus said to Pilate, 'My kingdom is not from this world' (John 18:36). Jesus engaged people's imaginations and stretched their ideas of the kingdom of God when he used images.

It was always an interesting exercise when I asked my students to share their images of God's kingdom. They would complete the statement, 'The kingdom of God is like …' using words or poetry or art. One wrote, 'The kingdom of God is like a family that adopts everyone who is alone.' Another said, 'The kingdom of God is like a diamond because it has many facets, it sparkles and attracts people and is valuable, but it is strong too and doesn't break.'

I would ask the students to imagine what a situation would be like if the values of the kingdom were lived by the people involved. Religious imagination is important. The famous artist, Norman Rockwell, painted many pictures that seemed ideal: the family gathered around the dinner table; the smiling grandfather and his grandson fishing together. Everyone in these paintings seemed to be happy and enjoying life and each other. The story is told that one of Rockwell's friends once told him that the trouble with his paintings was that they were too 'perfect'. The friend said that the way Rockwell painted life was not the way things really are. Rockwell responded to this by saying that he painted things that way intentionally. Things aren't as they could be, Rockwell felt, and by painting them better than they are, he hoped people could see the way things *could* be and perhaps act to make them better.

The kingdom was inaugurated in the incarnation of God's Son. The document on the Church, *Lumen Gentium*, says, 'This kingdom shone out before men in the word, in the works, and in the presence of Christ' (LG 5). The kingdom still shines forth in the Church and her members, as the Word of God is proclaimed and lived.

The kingdom shines in the Church as good works are done in Jesus' name and in Christ's presence in the sacraments and in the witness of the People of God.

What are the signs of the kingdom that we have experienced? At one time, the Pharisees asked Jesus when the kingdom of God was coming. Jesus answered them, 'The kingdom of God is not coming with things that can be observed; nor will they say, "Look, here it is!" or "There it is!" For, in fact, the kingdom of God is among you' (Luke 17:20-21).

I sometimes have to remind myself that the kingdom of God is already here, as well as still to come. It is important to remember that the kingdom is among us and to appreciate that gift.

The kingdom of God is already present in our families, in our schools and in our parishes. The *Catechism* says, 'The Church is the seed and beginning of this kingdom' (CCC 567). So we see the beginnings of the kingdom of God in the domestic church and in the faith community. We see, as we see in a flower seed, the potential for greater beauty as the seed unfolds.

Our vocation as catechists, whether parents or teachers, is part of the work of the kingdom of God. We proclaim the Word, do good works, receive the sacraments and witness to our beliefs. And we form others to do these things and to grow in their faith. Ours is an awesome vocation!

There are two lessons I learned about forming others in faith that have remained part of my life, though I learned them a very long time ago. The first lesson I learned when, as a young adult, I was asked to be a catechist. I was going to teach a group of nine-year-old children. I had never taught before, so I was very nervous, and I prepared mightily for that one-hour lesson.

When the day finally came for my teaching debut, the lesson went well. We gathered in prayer, we learned about Jesus and what he taught, we decided what we would do to live what Jesus asked and we prayed again and sent each other off on mission. I was pleased with the job I had done. I was proud.

As the students departed, I stood at the doorway saying goodbye. One of the students stopped and looked at me and said, 'You did pretty good'. I smiled, feeling, of course, that I had done well. 'Thanks', I replied. He began to move through the doorway and suddenly stopped again, turned around and said, 'By the way, when is the real teacher coming?'

Of course, we are all just stand-ins until the real Teacher comes, until he comes again. What that student reminded me was that, as I form others in faith, I have to be sure that I am faithful to the message of Jesus. He reminded me that this ministry is not mine, but belongs to Jesus and to his Church. I have to be sure

I know the message and that my teaching does what the Church asks that it do. I have to be rooted in Jesus and the community of faith.

I have held the lesson that student taught me as a foundation for all of my efforts to form others in faith. I am grateful to him. Indeed, sometimes, as Isaiah noted, 'a little child shall lead them'.

The other lesson I learned about being a catechist was from our son, Nick. At one point, I was not only Nick's mother, I was his religion teacher at school. It was easy to teach the lessons of Jesus about love and forgiveness to other people's children; those children went to their own homes after the lesson. But when I taught our son, he came home with me. He became a sort of 'living conscience' for me.

And when he did something wrong, or I was not in a good mood and was impatient, he would say, 'But today in class you said we should forgive and be patient with each other'. Nick was calling me to witness to what I had taught, as he had a right to expect I would.

Our own children certainly show us the truth of the need to 'practise what we preach'. The children we teach at school or in the parish look to us to do that too. That student and my son also reminded me that while we may be teachers, we are also learners and sometimes those we are forming in faith also form us in powerful ways.

The *General Directory* speaks eloquently of the vocation of the catechist and the ministry that catechesis does. It also speaks of our heritage of faith and lineage of catechists.

When catechesis transmits the mystery of Christ, the faith of the whole people of God echoes in its message throughout the course of history: the faith received by the Apostles from Christ himself and under the action of the Holy Spirit; that of the martyrs who bore witness to it and still bear witness to it by their blood; that of the saints who have lived it and live it profoundly; that of the Fathers and doctors of the Church who have taught it brilliantly; that of the missionaries who proclaim it incessantly; that of theologians who help to understand it better; that of pastors who conserve it with zeal and love and who interpret it authentically. In truth, there is present in catechesis the faith of all those who believe and allow themselves to be guided by the Holy Spirit. (GDC 105)

As parents and teachers, we are catechists who are part of the whole community of catechists that have served the Lord and God's people. I feel the presence of all those who have taught the faith surrounding and supporting my humble efforts.

And I celebrate all those who continue this work today in their homes and in our parishes and schools, whether they do so as parents or paid staff or volunteers. The kingdom grows through their – and your – efforts to nourish the gift of faith and to deepen in the hearts of your children their love for Jesus Christ.

The Prologue to the *Catechism of the Catholic Church* quotes the *Roman Catechism*, which says:

The whole concern of doctrine and its teaching must be directed to the love that never ends. Whether something is proposed for belief, for hope, or for action, the love of our Lord must always be made accessible, so that anyone can see that all the works of perfect Christian virtue spring from love and have no other objective than to arrive at love. (CCC Prologue 25)

The love that parents show for each other and for their children is holy. Love is shown in the simple, if not always easy, ways we live: by providing food and a safe home, caring for those who are ill or hurt and just being there to listen. We sacrifice for each other and each member contributes to the well-being of the family.

Teachers show love by offering a safe environment in which to learn and pray and share faith. They offer love when they give the encouragement, as well as the knowledge and skills they teach, that nourish their students.

When the parish is a loving community that offers loving welcome to all – even the outcasts and refugees and immigrants – we witness to the kingdom of God who is love.

When we live and love as Jesus asked us to do, then we are light for the world. Jesus told us the light of the world cannot be hidden and that it cannot be put under baskets of false humility or fear of failure; he said the light of the world is to be put on a stand so it can give light to all.

And Jesus tells us the reason we are to be light for the world, 'Let your light shine before others, so that they may see your good works and give glory to your Father in heaven' (Matthew 5:16).

I think of the parents and teachers I have known as being rainbow lights, recalling the promises of God. They show God's love and they witness to Jesus in the sometimes brilliant, sometimes muted, colours of daily life.

They show love with their eyes which see need, see discouragement, notice the child who needs extra attention or help, see the vision of who we can become. Parents and teachers show love with ears that listen to hopes and dreams; ears that really hear a person's worries; ears that hear questions as faith-seeking and not threatening.

Parents and teachers show love with mouths that smile, welcome and laugh; mouths that speak words of comfort when needed and challenge when necessary; mouths that admit failures and limitations.

Parents and teachers show love through their hands when they reach out to the outcast person, the marginalised child or the alienated adult. They show love with hands that gently touch the fearful person or the insecure person. They show love with arms that support those weary with responsibilities. They hold those who grieve and those who rejoice and sometimes catch those who fall.

Parents and teachers show love with their feet, which take them to wherever love is needed; they show love with feet that help them to lead the way, to run after lost sheep and to dance the dance of discipleship. You work the miracles of simply being present and generously offering love.

The more parents and teachers and the parish work together for the faith formation of adults, youth and children, the more effective that faith formation can be. The faith formation that we do at home is the foundation of what takes place in the parish and school formation.

Teachers need to recognise the holiness of families and the ordinary ways that families share faith and prayer and service.

And parents need to recognise that the community of faith that accepted their child at Baptism shares the responsibility to form that child in faith. We owe a debt of gratitude to those who build on what began and continues in our homes.

When our son was in the parish school, I was also on the faculty. For the first time I realised that we did not communicate as effectively as we could with parents. I knew the expectations the teachers had, not because they had told me their expectations for my role as a parent, but because I was on the faculty. I realised it would be helpful to both teachers and parents to communicate more regularly.

When I became a parish director of catechesis, I was surprised to discover that some of the parents and catechists had never even met each other. I began that year, and every year after, with a gathering of the parents and teachers. They met in small groups and shared their hopes and dreams for the children's growth in faith. Then they talked about the responsibilities of the home and the responsibilities of the parish and their expectations of one another. We shared refreshments and social time, and then prayed for each other and for the children.

Both parents and catechists loved the gatherings. It had opened lines of communication on a positive note. Catechists got to know which parents might be able to assist with a service project and which were willing to give a witness talk to the students about the ways they live their faith. Some parents offered special talents, like designing a set for the Scripture dramas the children performed or helping with music for prayer celebrations.

During the year, when a child did not come to class, I called to be sure the child was safe. I would say, 'Is Johnny alright? I just wanted you to know we miss him'. With my gentle opening, rather than an accusation like 'you didn't send your son to class', the parent would often respond with the story of all that was going on in the family: an illness, an accident, a job loss, a separation. These are the times the parish needs to reach out and help, not judge them. The same is true when parents do not make it to the meeting for their child's First Communion. Sometimes they are drowning in family crises and we add to their burden rather than help them to carry it.

The more parents and teachers worked together, the more our children seemed to grow – and we did too. Both parents and catechists were clear about their own roles and appreciative of the others' roles. We all realised that we are partners in this enterprise and that together we could do great works, as Jesus said those who believed in him would do.

Students whom I had taught when they were thirteen and fourteen years old celebrated the tenth anniversary of their graduation and invited the teachers who had taught them to attend. At one point in the evening, one of the former students came over to the faculty table and sat down with us. 'I want to tell you something', he said. 'When I was going to school here, my life was a mess. My parents were going through a divorce and they were hurting and angry. I was shuffled from one parent to the other, and I was confused about a lot of things. I had no one to talk to. My parents were too busy with their own problems. And I would come to school and you all loved me. You listened and taught me what was right and what was wrong. You helped me and guided me. And what I want to tell you is, you saved my life.' Then he paused, and finally spoke again, saying, 'Now, I have a little boy of my own and I am going to save his life like you saved mine'.

You are saving lives with every lesson you teach, at home or in class. You are saving lives with every tear you dry and every wound – of body, of spirit, of heart – you tend to. You are saving lives with each word of kindness you offer, with every word of compassion you whisper and with the precious moments of listening that you do. You are saving lives in this life and into the life of the kingdom of God.

Faith is a gift and that gift enables us to work for the kingdom of God even when things do not go well. There was a man who lived in the parish where I taught. His wife and children were Catholic, but he did not believe in God. He was a doctor and each year he would go to a very poor country and offer free medical care for the children in some area there. I asked him to speak about this work to our older children and their families at our annual Lenten gathering. It was a moving presentation, as my students and their families saw pictures of young people, the same age as the students, who were malnourished and had deformed arms and legs. Some of those children in the photos, who were in their early teens, could only crawl because their bones had not formed properly. All of those present were changed by the doctor's presentation and lived that Lent differently.

When the doctor had finished the presentation that evening and the people had all left, he said to me, 'I envy you'. I was taken aback by his remark and asked why. 'Because', he said, 'you don't always need to see results. I depend on the results I can see – when I can fix a child's leg and I see him walk again, or I fix the bone in a woman's arm and I see her hold her baby again. I need to see that I have made something better and that I have made a difference. Because you have faith, you don't need to see results, do you? You can see more: you see that you are a part of something bigger that your God does and so you don't need to see the results yourself. You have that faith and trust that you are making a difference even when you can't see it. I wish I had what you have.'

That man hungered to have faith, and eventually found it – or it found him. Witnessing the gratitude and joy that he had because he was able to believe made me realise again what a gift faith is. It is a gift that calls for a response that we must make each day and that we help one another to make. It is the response to God's gift that we help our children to make as we form them to live that faith.

The hunger for faith and spirituality is much more 'out in the open', much more public than it was when I was young. Libraries and bookstores have shelf upon shelf of religion and spirituality books. There are thousands of sites on the internet that address spirituality and religion. And people travel all over the world to places where there have been apparitions of Mary, or places of devotion of some sort. If any of these – books, the web or journeys – make one more loving towards God and neighbour, I guess they are helpful. But sometimes the hunger for faith goes deep and the things people seek will not satisfy that hunger. On one internet auction site, a toasted cheese sandwich which claimed to 'have the image of the Virgin Mary' on it sold for $28,000 in the US. People buy things and travel far and wide to find the holy. Have they lost sight of the fact – or forgotten – that the kingdom of God is among us?

Parents and teachers help us to see and to remember the holiness that is present all around us. They help us to grow in holiness and to spread the kingdom of God.

For Reflection

What image would you use for the kingdom of God?

Who helps you to remember that the kingdom of God is among us?

What lessons have you learned from children?

Chapter X

'The harvest is plentiful'
(Matthew 9:37)

The *General Directory for Catechesis* uses the Scripture story that Jesus told about the sower and seed as an image for catechesis. You remember the story, the sower seems to indiscriminately throw the seed and it lands in various places. Some seed fell on rocky ground and it sprouted, but, having no depth of soil, it died; some fell among thorns, so when it grew it was choked by the thorns; and some fell on good soil and it grew and increased and yielded a hundred fold.

When we sow the seed of God's Word, we have to know the ground where we sow it. That is to say, we have to know the people we are forming and the reality of their lives since 'every dimension of the faith, like the faith itself as a whole, must be rooted in human experience' (GDC 87). We have to be aware of the culture of the people, their nationality and the societal culture in which they live. And we must discern in these cultures 'which riches to "take" up as compatible with the faith; on the other hand, it must seek to "purify" and "transform" those criteria, modes of thought and lifestyles which are contrary to the Kingdom of God' (GDC 109). In every culture, there are seeds of the gospel already present, which must be nourished and cared for. In every culture there are weeds, which are contrary to the gospel and, if faith is to grow, must be eradicated or transformed. For example, culture might promote generosity and that is to be embraced. That same culture might promote excessive consumerism and materialism that are contrary to the gospel and must be called to transformation.

The *General Directory* analyses the 'soil' of the world today in which we sow the gospel message. It calls our attention to some realities that concern all of us: human rights and attacks on the dignity of the person; the impact of science and technology on people's lives; religious indifference and atheism.

There are other world issues and cultural realities that we must be aware of, other issues that affect the soil in which we sow the word. There are natural disasters, ecological and environmental issues, war and terrorism, economic issues and failures in corporations, governments and even in the Church itself.

What issues and concerns directly impact your children and their families? Is the impact a positive one or a negative one? If we do not know the 'soil' of the lives of those whom we catechise, we will not be able to proclaim the word in ways that is Good News. We will not know how to encourage the growth of the seeds of the gospel that are present or recognise the weeds of anti-gospel attitudes that need to be pulled.

I believe the parable of the sower has something else to say to us as parents and teachers. I picture the sower generously throwing handfuls of seeds, scattering them as he walked along. Sometimes people seem to fence off their little area, whether that area is their family or their ministry or their organisation. They alone are allowed to sow in that area; but they do not have any interest in sowing beyond their own area either.

In one parish, the person in charge of liturgy and the person in charge of religious education refused to work together. It was common knowledge that you could be friends with one of them, but you could not befriend both of them. The effect was that these ministries became separate fiefdoms and so the community's formation in faith was lopsided.

This kind of attitude inhibits the spread of the gospel. Jesus certainly did not limit his proclamation of the Good News to one little field or deny anyone else the opportunity to participate in the sowing. The more generously we sow the Good News, and the more we do so cooperatively, the better chance it has of growing.

When I had a garden, I began to understand how seeds grow and what they need. I soon also learned that whatever my neighbours allowed to grow in their yard would eventually come over to grow in mine too – for better or for worse. Whatever we sow in life will touch our neighbours and their children too.

In our efforts to sow the seed of the gospel and to help it grow in our lives and the lives of our children, we may become discouraged in the face of all the troubles in the world, in our own countries and communities. Sometimes the terrible events that are happening can overwhelm us and make us weary.

Jesus must have gotten weary sometimes and even overwhelmed at the needs he saw. The Gospel of Matthew says:

> Jesus went about all the cities and villages, teaching in their synagogues, and proclaiming the good news of the kingdom, and curing every disease and sickness. When he saw the crowds, he had compassion for them, because they were harassed and helpless, like sheep without a shepherd. (Matthew 9:35-36)

It sounds overwhelming to me: the travelling and the preaching, the healing and the awareness of the crowd's needs. Yet, it is right after this that Jesus said to his disciples, 'The harvest is plentiful'. We sometimes look at the needs of the world and see them as destroying the harvest. Jesus looked at the needs of his world and saw the potential harvest. Every need is an opportunity to respond with the Good News in word and deed. Every need calls forth the sowing of a response that will bear fruit. And so the harvest begins.

I believe the harvest is still plentiful; the potential for the gospel to touch people's lives even amid the problems of the world is great. But then the harvest needs labourers. Jesus said that we should ask the Lord to send labourers. Perhaps you and I are the answer to someone's prayer for the labourers to be sent. But still more labourers are needed – they are always needed if the kingdom is to grow.

It reminds me of the story about the preacher whose congregation was becoming apathetic and unmotivated. So one day he preached a sermon to rouse them. He began saying quietly and softly, 'My people, there are so many needs we see around us, and such hunger for the Good News. We must be willing to leave this sanctuary and to bring the Good News beyond these walls and into our neighbourhood. So, let the church walk!' To which the people responded, 'Amen, brother, let the church walk!' With a bit more drama and fire in his voice, the preacher went on, 'But there are needs beyond our neighbourhood. We see the people of our city in fear and they are lost and alone. We see the people of this city living in poverty and they are desperate for the Good News. We must leave this place to go beyond our neighbourhood and to the city to be Good News. So, let the church run!' And the congregation was caught up in the preacher's urgent plea and they shouted, 'Amen, brother, let the church run!' Then the preacher grew louder and more passionate, and he shouted back to them, 'But we are to go to all the world and to proclaim the Good News to all those in need, so, let the church fly!' And the people eagerly shouted, 'Amen, brother, let the church fly!' Then the preacher, at fever pitch, exclaimed, 'This mission to all people will need each one of you. It will require that you give your time, your talents and your significant financial contributions, so, let the church soar!' To which the congregation quickly replied, 'Then let the church walk'.

We can, and should, pray that the Lord of the harvest send more labourers into the fields, but we have to labour too. It will, as the preacher said, take every one of us. It will require our time, talents and treasure.

How is Jesus asking us to use these gifts for his mission? In the Old Testament, people are often called by God to leave their homes in order to be his prophets or to lead in his name. Jesus called people into discipleship and they left their old lives behind. The author Henri Nouwen wrote about the 'displacement' to which we are called as disciples. This does not necessarily mean leaving our homes, but rather calls us to be ready to go beyond our comfort zone in order to carry on the work of Jesus.

When I was a teacher in the parish school, I was asked by Sister Carolyn, the director of the parish religious education programmes, to speak to her catechists. I said no. She persisted and I asked what she thought I could say to them. She said I had good ways of teaching religion; I said I was sure the catechists had their own ways. She still persisted and, because she was my friend, I finally acquiesced. I was to speak to eight catechists for forty minutes. I think I put in at least eighteen hours of preparation and I felt ill and didn't sleep well for the entire week before the event. I was called beyond my comfort zone and learned that God would be with me when I ventured out.

We do not move beyond our comfort zone for the sake of moving, but in order to do the mission of Jesus and to do it more effectively. A school principal who was retiring once said proudly, 'For twenty-six years I have maintained the status quo'. I suppose in some situations maintaining the status quo is an achievement, but I had to wonder if that was the case, or if she had simply found her own comfort zone and set up camp. And I found myself questioning whether she evaluated the religion programme or measured its effectiveness in any way. And I wondered if she did do these things and there was never any need to adjust anything or to try a new way.

There are various ways to do faith formation in our homes, and different models or schedules that are used in schools and parishes. Whatever the particular model or materials used, we have a responsibility to ensure that a holistic formation is offered. A holistic formation attends to the six dimensions: knowledge, prayer, liturgy, morality, community and mission. And we have to ensure that these dimensions are faithfully and adequately addressed in age-appropriate ways.

As parents, we might move beyond our comfort zone of memorised prayer and introduce spontaneous prayer with our children. In class, we might try using a meditation with children. Parishes might send home or post on the parish website some thoughts for families to discuss in preparation for the Sunday liturgy.

When we are discouraged, we can recall the Scripture story of the disciples who had fished all night and caught nothing. Then Jesus came and told them, 'Put out into deep water', and they caught so many fish their nets were beginning to break. Jesus will help us to see how to fish for people in a better way and he will keep our hope alive.

In a world where bad things happen daily and leaders fail us, cynicism is a popular posture. Often when people are hopeful, they are dismissed as Pollyannas. Being cynical seems to be considered wise. The people who see the bright side of things are judged as simple at best, ignorant or even worse. But hope is not a personality trait; it is a theological virtue and a discipline of faith.

I heard many stories of people who survived the devastating earthquake in Haiti, but one in particular has stayed with me. The man who had been rescued was a concert violinist who was blind. By the time they finally dug him out of the rubble, he had been buried there for over eighteen hours. The news cameras were there capturing the rescue.

A few days later, the rescued man was being interviewed as he lay on a cot in a makeshift hospital. He was asked how he kept hope alive during the eighteen-hour ordeal. He kept hope alive, he explained, with his music. He played his violin in his imagination – Tchaikovsky, Brahms, Mozart – over and over. As he played the music, the music moved him to prayer. He gave thanks, in his grave of debris, for all that Jesus Christ had done for him, and he remembered and recounted each blessing in his prayer of gratitude. By then the rescuers were digging near him and he could hear them. And, he prayed to Jesus, 'If I survive, tell me what I should do'. He heard an answer and was determined that if he survived, he would do what Jesus asked. And, as he lay in the hospital, wounded but healing, he was already making plans. He would rebuild the music school that had been destroyed in the earthquake and he would teach children to play music.

That man's story of hope reminds me of the ways that we offer hope through faith formation. We teach the symphony of faith, and then our people can hear it echo wherever they are. We have taught them to participate in the Mass and sacraments, and they hear the strains of the symphony in a deeper way and encounter the Composer. We teach them to pray and they learn to give thanks for blessings and to ask for help and guidance. We teach them morality and they learn to choose to do what Jesus asks; we teach them to serve the community and so they plan and build and make the world more like the kingdom of God.

Faith formation enables us to be people of hope and to help our children to be hopeful. We can find hope – and help our children to find it – in little things, like making up with a friend after a disagreement.

We might see hope when someone finally masters a skill that one had failed at before. We can find and share the hope that comes in big ways: a successful cancer treatment or the end of a conflict somewhere in the world. We can pass on stories of hope instead of the ones that lead to despair.

We are the people of God, the people of the Paschal Mystery, and anything less than hope is unworthy of those who follow the Lord, who overcame even death. We have all known times when we died in a little way – a failure, a loss – and we have known the joy of rising again to overcome the failure, to be at peace with the loss. All of these are stories of hope that we can share with each other and with our children. In the face of enormous problems, when we are saying to ourselves that we simply can't solve them all, hope enables us to not give up; hope enables us, with God's grace, to do what we can do and to trust that that is enough.

We find hope as we live and share the gospel. To find hope requires that we live the faith and teach it faithfully and continue to learn about and grow in faith ourselves so that we remain always true to the gospel.

Once I worked with a teacher who I heard say to the students, 'That part of the book is wrong'. When I later inquired as to what exactly was 'wrong', the teacher pointed to the book and to the page on which it told about Jesus quoting the prophet Isaiah's words, 'The Spirit of the Lord is upon me, because he has anointed me to bring good news to the poor'. 'That part of the book is wrong', the teacher told his students. Perhaps the fact that this teacher was very wealthy influenced his judgement; our own lifestyles may lead us to misinterpret what Jesus says.

I participated with a small group of adults from my parish in a Scripture sharing group. We would gather in one of our homes, pray together and reflect on the readings for the coming Sunday. One week, we were sharing our thoughts on the story of the rich young man. We read from the Gospel of Mark that Jesus said to the man, 'You lack one thing; go, sell what you own, and give the money to the poor, and you will have treasure in heaven; then come, follow me' (Mark 10:21).

Someone in the group asked, 'What do you think Jesus meant when he said, "Sell what you own, and give the money to the poor"?' Various members responded. One said, 'Well, of course, we have to provide for our families and have something set aside for our own needs, then we should give to the poor.' Another suggested, 'We should be sure to have enough for our children's education and to cover medical bills and then, of course, we should give to the poor.' Finally, someone asked me directly what I thought Jesus meant. 'I think', I said, 'he meant, "Go, sell what you own, and give the money to the poor".' There was an audible gasp from some in the group. 'Understand', I continued, 'I have not done this. I try every day to be less concerned with money and possessions, but I am not willing to change Jesus' words to accommodate my lifestyle.'

The gospel message transforms us; we do not change the gospel to fit our needs or to say what we would like it to say. As disciples, we continue to hold to the ideal of discipleship, all the while accepting and supporting and loving each other, even though we do not always measure up. Both the gospel ideal, which we hold up and teach, and the journey with one another towards living that ideal more fully can bring hope.

We have the hope that comes to us from the Holy Spirit. The *General Directory* reminds us, 'Neither catechesis nor evangelisation is possible without the action of God working through his Spirit. In catechetical praxis neither the most advanced pedagogical techniques nor the most talented catechist can ever replace the silent and unseen action of the Holy Spirit' (GDC 288). This is not to say that the talents of the catechist – parent or teacher – are not important. It is not to say that the techniques we use to catechise make no difference. It simply assures us that the Holy Spirit will inspire our efforts.

My husband, Ray, once shared with me the image that he had of the working of the Holy Spirit. It is like being at a very young child's birthday party. The birthday cake is brought in with its candles lighted. One of the child's parents will take the child onto his or her lap, sitting with the child as the birthday cake is set before them. Then the child is told to make a wish and blow out the candles. The parent knows that the little child cannot blow them out alone. So, as the child blows, the parent adds his or her own breath, and the candles go out. The child would fail with only its own breath and no parent would blow the candles out unless the child was blowing too. Therefore, Ray believes, we cannot do our work alone, but our efforts are essential. The breath of the Spirit makes our efforts strong enough to do the mission.

As parents and teachers, we know the Spirit works in and through us when we are responsive to the inspiration the Spirit offers. Have you ever had to talk with your children about something important and you don't know how you will tell them, and as you are talking the right words come to you and you don't know where they came from? Well, actually, we do know where they came from.

When I do catechesis with adults, I ask them to name someone who helped them to grow in faith, and most frequently they will name a parent or a teacher. The children entrusted to you may one day gather as adults and may be asked that same question – and it will be you they name.

Then the adults share the ways in which the person they named helped them to grow in faith and the first answer is always about the way that person was like Jesus in their words and actions, their witness of life. Other ways that the person helped them to grow in faith reflect the six dimensions of faith formation in some way: the person taught them about God or taught them to pray or took them to Mass and the sacraments. They may say the person helped them to understand right and wrong and to make good choices. They may name the sense of belonging to the Church community that that person helped them to understand, or the service they did together to spread the Good News of Jesus Christ.

My husband had a wonderful question he would pose to me when I got frantic about some inconsequential task. 'Sweetie', he would ask, 'forty-four years from now will it make any difference?' His question helped me to see what was of lasting value and what was not.

Forty-four years from now, the faith formation that you do will make all the difference: for our families, our communities, the Church and the world. Because of your faith, and with God's grace, some people will come to know Jesus better or will begin a journey of faith. Some adults will deepen their faith because of you, and children and youth will grow towards maturity of faith. People who suffer will be comforted and those who are tempted will be strengthened. Some who were alienated will come home to Christ and the Church.

Let us pray, for each other and for all parents and teachers, that we might follow the last words of Mary recorded in Scripture, 'Do whatever he tells you'.

For Reflection

The harvest needs labourers. Think of someone you will mentor to be a teacher of faith – then do it!

How is Jesus asking you to 'leave home', to go beyond your comfort zone to teach the faith to your children?

The first letter of Peter says, 'Always be ready to make your defence to anyone who demands from you an account of the hope that is in you' (1 Peter 3:15). Think of the reasons for your hope. Share your reasons for hope with someone – and keep sharing!